All Things Consoled

A daughter's memoir

ELIZABETH
HAY

McClelland & Stewart

Library and Archives Canada Cataloguing in Publication data
is available upon request

ISBN: 978-0-7710-3973-7
ebook ISBN: 978-0-7710-3974-4

Typeset in Bembo by M&S, Toronto
Printed and bound in the USA

McClelland & Stewart,
a division of Penguin Random House Canada Limited,
a Penguin Random House Company
www.penguinrandomhouse.ca

1   2   3   4   5   22   21   20   19   18

For my dear friend Sheila McCook,
who knows the score.

All Things Consoled

HER KNEE

THEIR LIVES CAME TUMBLING down during that Indian summer in 2008 when Obama won for the first time and the world seemed bright with second chances. The morning after the election, a Wednesday, I went to do errands in the sunshine, returning home in the early afternoon to a message on the answering machine. His spine-straightening voice, the basso profundo that used to make students snap to attention from Georgian Bay to Whirl Creek: "Liz. Call your dad as soon as you can."

I reached him. Without preamble, he said, "An ambulance has come to take your mom—"

His voice cracked. He broke off. I couldn't speak either, torn into by what he was saying. Their telephone sat on a low countertop beside the refrigerator. He must have been standing there, struggling to master his emotions, receiver to his ear, his face working against him. And then he found a way out. "Would you like to talk to Toula?"

Toula was the nurse in their neighbourhood clinic. I knew her by reputation. My mother had mentioned her more than once, enchanted by her combination of warmth, stylish good looks, utter competence. The painter in my mother dwelled especially on Toula's striking brown eyes, so intelligent and alive. There was a long wait. I heard sets of footsteps in the hallway, directions being given. Finally Toula's voice in my ear. She said she had arrived to find my mother unable to get out of bed, "Very, very weak, probably dehydrated. She hasn't been eating. She's looking extremely frail right now." There were no beds in the hospital, Toula went on, so she would be admitted through emergency and might be there for a couple of days while she was assessed. "Maybe with some extra fluid she'll feel much better." She paused and her voice changed as she expressed the bigger problem. "I'm very concerned long-term about how they'll cope at home."

So was I. So was I.

I asked her how my father was and again she paused. "He's at a loss," she said.

That evening my husband, Mark, and I set out from Ottawa on the seven-hour drive across Ontario to London, the medium-sized city in the southwestern corner of the province where my parents had lived for nearly forty years. We drove until after midnight, located a roadside inn, slept as best we could, had an early breakfast and continued on. A bit before eight o'clock, we rang my father's doorbell and stepped inside. Down the stairs he came in his thick sweater, patched pants, eternal dark-blue beanie on his bald head, all smiles and relief at the sight of us. The hospital had called two hours earlier, asking permission to operate on my mother's infected left knee.

I expressed my bewilderment. "But on Saturday she sounded well!"

"She was," Dad said. "I thought everything was going fine." But on Tuesday evening, as Obama's victory was announced over the radio—my parents had no television—she stood up from the chesterfield and fell three times trying to get to the bedroom. "I thought I was stronger. I had a hell of a time getting her up."

Shoving his hands into his pockets, fixing his eyes on the carpet, "This can't go on."

We drove to the hospital and found my mother hooked up to an IV pole and lying on a bed in the emergency ward with an intern beside her, taking her blood. She was feistier and more coherent than I had expected; the extra fluid had done its good work. The young intern, examining her parchment-like old hand with its big purple veins, muttered, "Lots of veins here." And my mother quipped, "Veins, but no vanity."

To us she said, "There's only one word for this: *helldamnspit*." A salty bit of invective she credited to her roommate at the Toronto General when they were nurses-in-training. A Maritimer, she added with fondness, as if only a Maritimer would be so colourful and apt.

I was always impressed by my mother, never more so than now. She had no fear and no self-pity, or none that I could see. Part of it was her hospital training, but most of it was her calm and measured outlook on life and death. She was an artist, creative in every bone of her body, yet the most practical of women. There was nothing she could not do with her hands, and she was knowledgeable and smart.

A doctor came by eventually. He couldn't say how the infection had come about, he didn't know. "Bacteria got into her bloodstream," he said simply.

I was intent on telling him about the extensive dental work she had undergone on three consecutive Thursdays, ending exactly one week ago. He shrugged. "Dentists say we blame everything on them. There are many sources of bacteria—skin, mouth. What's important is that the infection in her knee not travel to the artificial hip, which has all sorts of nooks and crannies and is much harder to clean up."

After an hour or so, Mark took my father home and I stayed on with my mother while she waited to be wheeled to an operating room. Having foreseen that there would be many hours of waiting, I had brought along her copy of *Moby-Dick*, the book she had taken to with a vengeance in her early eighties, reading it from start to finish three times. "Not *every* page," I had said to her skeptically, and she had looked me in the eye and said, "Not only every page, but every *word* on every page." While we waited, I read her the first two chapters and together we were drawn into that gnarled and watery world of long ago when language breathed the life of sailing ships and the sea, and when nature in the form of a white whale capsized everything and everyone.

The next morning, two physiotherapists came into her room and got her up and shuffling on a walker, still attached to her IV pole, around the bed and over to a chair. One of them said she was a tough cookie, and my mother had a quick comeback: "I've been baked a long time." Later, when the same fellow returned to move her back to her bed, he got entangled with the IV pole. "These accoutrements get in the way," he apologized, and my mother replied, "That's French. And I don't have a riposte."

She had always had a quick wit and a way with words when the mood took her. So when I say, as I tend to do, that I don't come from a line of storytellers, that silence held sway in my parents' house because they were quiet people, I'm not really to be believed.

That morning she was certainly all there, and yet she was elsewhere. In bed she raised her arm as if holding a paintbrush, blocking something off, and remarked that the diagonal (formed by the curtain rods) was interfering with her painting.

The work so much on her mind was what she called her sawmill quartet. They were paintings based on a photograph she had taken years ago inside an abandoned sawmill my parents had come upon on one of their drives through small-town Ontario, my father behind the wheel, my mother ever alert beside him. In the photograph a shaft of light poured through a dusty window into the dark interior of the mill and shone on a massive circular blade with jagged teeth and a vertical steel guiding arm. Sawdust lay thick and gleaming on diagonal boards next to the saw, much as if straw had been spun into gold overnight.

She told me she had some touching up to do, some correcting, and she had to cook the surface. Then she stopped herself and sighed. "We can't do everything we want to do in our lives. That's greediness."

A pair of friends arrived, bringing flowers. They had known my parents a long time, had curled with them in the winter and canoed with them in the summer. They asked my mother how she was feeling and she said, "Strange." But when they asked if she had given up painting, she declared, roused to certitude and volubility, "Not a bit of it." She launched into a description of a second series of paintings, companions to the sawmill quartet. "We used to have a beautiful black cherry tree in the garden. It came down one winter," she said, "leaving a large black stump, and the next autumn I went out into the garden and saw three scarlet maple leaves on the stump, perfectly arranged. I thought, I cannot, cannot, *cannot* resist painting this." Both series flowed from the same fascination with colour, composition and her concern for the Canadian forest and the future of the natural world: the maple leaves like jewels on the black stump, the darkness of the sawmill, the torturing teeth of the blades, the open question about how many beautiful autumns we had left. "This is what I have on my back now," she said to them.

I've condensed and abbreviated her explanations and aspirations here, because at this stage in her life—she was about to turn eighty-nine—she was more often than not laboured and repetitive when she talked about her work, so repetitive and obsessed, in fact, that she wore my father's patience raw. He had muttered to me that if the gallery curator my mother relied on did not accept these final paintings, there would be hell to pay.

When I got back from the hospital in the late afternoon, I went out into her studio, built onto the side of the house, and looked around for the four sawmill paintings. One was balanced on her big easel; the other three were stacked on the floor nearby. To my dismay all of them were rudimentary and lifeless, not nearly as good as the photograph itself. I was used to seeing works in progress that made me doubt her talent, only to find in the finished canvas a unity and confidence that made me think her remarkable. With these sawmill paintings, however, there was only uninspired copying on view. She's too old, I thought. She can't do it anymore. The curator won't want these. And I felt heartsick for my mother and embarrassed, and ashamed of my embarrassment.

That evening we were in touch with my brothers and sister, planning out when they would come: my botanist brother in Montreal, my oceanographer brother in Halifax, my musician sister in Mexico City. Stuart, Alex, Jeannie. A flower and fern man, a sand and tides man, a clarinetist.

The next morning my father broke down when he talked about why my mother's paintings meant so much to her. "It's because you've all done so well." His face crumpled; he wept. "She never had the chance," he managed to say finally, "she never had the chance to go to university. So her paintings are her way of showing off. That's why they mean so much to her, *I* think."

He was understanding her on his own competitive terms, which meant he wasn't understanding her at all, it seemed to me. I changed my mind later, when a social worker came by to sort out what would be needed when my mother came home, and she paused to appreciate all the paintings on the walls. I explained that my mother was the artist, and my father said, "Painting is her reason for existence." He spoke in his definitive way, a schoolmaster brooking no argument.

A year before, I had received an email asking me if I was Gordon Hay's daughter. The correspondent had been a junior teacher at the high school in Guelph, the small city near London, where my father had taught in the late 1960s. She wrote, "Gordon Hay, also a history teacher, was tall, very intelligent, distinguished, well-dressed in tweed jackets, with a briefcase, greying, had a powerful deep voice, and a wonderful twinkle in his eyes when he smiled."

The other side of Dad, I thought at the time, the public side. At his tallest as a young man, he was five feet ten, but he carried himself well and came across as tall. With the junior teacher he would have been supportive, interested, eager to tease, delighted if she responded in kind, a professionally confident man of fifty who was still setting his sights on bigger things. His younger colleague was remembering what I tended to forget—reminding me that my view of him was too narrow. Hers wasn't the only letter I had received from someone who appreciated him; former students had written to me too. My own description of him would have been so much more critical, as would his. So I treasured what she said, and felt chastened.

Now in his late eighties he was an old man. While my mother was in the hospital, he took to sleeping in a sleeping bag, laying it across the bare mattress of their fine old mahogany bed. I offered to make up the bed for him and he refused, saying, "That's fine. I don't want sheets." Since my father never said anything he did not mean, I let it go, but the makeshift look of the bed added to the atmosphere of crisis and mild insanity that pervaded the house. Even after my mother returned from the hospital and we installed her in the spare bedroom across the hall, my father did not want his bed made up. It took me a while to understand why. He and my mother had always slept close, wrapped around each other, so inside a sleeping bag he must have felt less adrift. And wasn't it also true that his life had become unmoored, and he might as well admit it?

Stu and Al arrived from Montreal and Halifax while my mother was still in the hospital. They spent the morning with her, and I went to see her in the afternoon. To my eyes she looked beautiful and dying. It took such an effort for her to hold up her head that I was reminded of Jet, the black Lab we grew up with, losing the same battle at the end of his life. The gauntness of my mother's face, her white hair (after I brushed and combed it), and her high cheekbones made her look leonine. The resident doctor said she had come into the hospital with considerable pneumonia. The strep bacteria had entered her bloodstream by way of her lungs and travelled to her knee, where it seeded out, as he put it, gathering there and going to town. For his part, the surgeon warned us that the infection might storm back, despite the antibiotics being pumped into her system. If so, he would be able to operate one more time. After that, he would have to install an artificial knee. And beyond that, he would have to amputate the leg.

At home my father freely admitted that he could not look after her anymore. "We should dispose of the paintings," he said, "sell the house and get accommodation in Ottawa."

Ottawa, because some years earlier Mark and I had suggested they move here, where we could help them out if they needed it, and surely they would, given my mother's bad hip and shoulder and my father's dependence on her for his meals. They had seemed open to the idea and grateful, and said they would think about it. A month or so later, in a telephone call, my father said, "Your mother and I have talked it over and we are going to stay here. Period. End of discussion."

The telephone did not bring out the best in my father. Never mind. I was relieved. The move was really Mark's idea, not mine; he was the generous one. I said our offer remained open if ever they changed their minds.

Now he said vehemently, "There's nothing to keep us in London."

No move could happen, however, until my mother was well enough to travel. Over the next few weeks my brothers and I and my sister (who also flew in to be with them) watched her knee, looking for signs of the infection's return, for reddening, swelling, fever. In the meantime Mark visited retirement homes in Ottawa, and at night we talked on the telephone, trying to plan ahead without knowing the future.

Kind neighbours brought meals to us. One of them spoke about how connected my mother and father were to the community. She referred to my father's lawn bowling, said he was always out in the garden, said she was used to seeing him drive by in his sporty red car, wearing his beret. But when I relayed her words to him and asked if he wasn't going to miss these ties in London, he snorted in derision: "To think we have lots of friends is utter nonsense. As far as I'm concerned, we're friendless. Has the phone been ringing? Has anybody been knocking on the door?"

My father turned eighty-nine while my mother was still in the hospital. By this time Al was staying with him and I was back home in Ottawa. I telephoned Dad to wish him a happy birthday, and his reaction would have done Eeyore proud. "*Happy*," he spat out, as if the word were a sour joke.

A week later, when my mother came home, it happened to be my turn in London, so I heard her declare, "I'm going to get better. I didn't think I was. I'd lost all incentive." She was fervently glad to be in her own house again.

In the spare bedroom, looking east, the Christmas cactus was all abloom in the corner of the bright window. Every night at bedtime my father prepared a hot water bottle for her (just as every morning his father, Conran, had taken Gracie, Dad's mother, a cup of tea in bed). He filled it partway with steaming, not boiling, water from the kettle, then folded it over to expel the air, put in the stopper and slipped the whole into a hand-sewn sleeve. He took it down the hall to where she lay in bed, and with exclamations of gratitude she positioned it on her lower belly and upper thighs, where the veins, she said, went down the legs.

Beside her in bed was a saucepan that she hit with a spoon whenever she needed the commode at night. And so at random intervals, clanging rang out through the dark house and I went to her, not always in time. There was one middle-of-the-night when I thought she had lost her mind. "What is this?" she said with a wild look in her eye, lifting and picking at the blanket.

"It's too heavy. What's this?" Picking at the flannel sheet underneath her. "This?" Clutching and picking at the upper sheet, until she lay back exhausted, frantic. "I can't get comfortable. It's too heavy. I can't get warm. If they weren't so *heavy*," her mouth dryly formed the words, "then I could sleep."

I refilled her hot water bottle and tried to settle her down. Back in my own bed in the adjoining room, I lay dismayed and frightened, then went in to her again and put my arms around her. "Are you all right now? Are you warm now?" And she was more herself, sorry for the trouble she was causing.

"Now I'm worried about you," she said. "We're sucking the life out of you."

And so it felt. I was in dangerous personal territory, a fraught border country in which my parents were sliding into neediness and I was rising to power, yet losing my own life.

On the telephone, after my parents were in bed, I spoke in a guarded voice to Mark, hyper-aroused by the difficulties I saw ahead, first of sleeping, then of caring for my mother and father over the next month or so, and then over the years in Ottawa. "What are we getting ourselves into?" I said, haunted by the fate of a dear friend whose mother had lived to be 106, unless it was 107.

Mark laughed with easy warmth and said we had to embrace life. "Take it on," he said. "You can't run from it." Putting my mind at rest in the moment.

But taking care of people has never been my idea of embracing life. On the contrary, it's the best way to ruin it.

So why did I do it, I ask myself looking back, and the answers come, one after the other. I wanted to look after my mother; I wanted to prove that I could be generous for once in my life; I saw no alternative. But something else was going on too, namely sibling rivalry and pride. The child's need, my need, to be the one who mattered most. I also wanted the credit. I've always wanted the credit. My name on the book. Let's all clap for Lizzie.

One afternoon I went for a walk through the silent, empty neighbourhood. No one was about except for two small, listless children in snowsuits lying on their stomachs in their front yard, building something, perhaps. One called plaintively to the other, who refused to do as bidden, and soon they would both be back inside, that was a certainty. The neighbourhood had been near-countryside forty years before when my parents built their house overlooking fields and trees, only for the land to fill up, year by year, with cookie-cutter mansions; godawful travesties, my mother called them. For me it was the outer armpit of the world, a suburb distant from downtown, an isolated tract of three-car garages with my parents' single-car garage and house of normal proportions the exception to the rule.

I came in from my walk and my parents brightened at the sight of my rosy cheeks. No greater gift to them existed than a set of rosy, healthy cheeks on any of their children.

That evening my father continued his ongoing lament about being friendless. "Bill would have been over a dozen times. Bill would have been over every day. Okay."

Okay meaning: That's all I have to say. End of conversation.

Bill, his buddy from across the street, had died about ten years before, a gregarious, clever man who loved dogs, loved fishing, enjoyed my mother and befriended my father. My father had no such aptitude for reaching out the hand of friendship. "The last friend I had was Ed Stevens," he said.

"We have no close friends." And then again, "Nobody's come to see us."

The fact is, he did not let people know about my mother's illness. Oh, a few. But he loathed the telephone. When two women friends of my mother's came to see her, he beat a hasty retreat to his bedroom and did not come out until they had left.

An attentive neighbour came over one day, laden down with an enormous lasagna, many butter tarts, wine, bountiful grapes. Tom carried the food into the kitchen, then went down the hall to see my mother. Later, I told her about all the food he had brought to us, and she smiled. "So kind of them. That's the Irish in them," she said.

"Do you know why I'm not sleeping?" she said to me later. "Because I've been *painting*. It occurs to me, those embroidered linen handkerchiefs—they would be a marvellous background for the pieces of lichen on rock. The point is the age, the length of time it takes nature to make the lichen on the one hand, and for women to make the linen and the embroidery on the other."

Propped up now against several pillows in bed, the wooden-legged tray across her lap, she wet her middle fingertip on her tongue and picked up every crumb, one by three, off the folded napkin that had held an oatmeal cookie, her mug of coffee next to it doctored with cream from a carton of whipping cream and reheated an infinite number of times. "Give it the one-two-three," she would say, instructing me to return the mug to the microwave and press those numbers. No hot drink was satisfactory unless it took the roof off the top of her mouth.

I remarked that she was happy with her cookie, and my father, sitting in a chair on the far side of the bed, said, "I've never seen your mother unhappy."

It took me a moment to absorb this pronouncement. It was hard to believe that he knew her so little.

"Well," she said, "if I tell you the truth, and I always do, there's a lot of play-acting."

"I know," my father said. "But I've never seen you in tears."

I had seen bouts of tears overpower her mighty resistance many times. When music moved her, or when the family gathered at home or at the lake and she felt overcome by her good fortune, or when she defended Dad and testified to their love for me. I had seen her weeping in the kitchen after Gracie died, a mother-in-law she loved and felt loved by far more than by her own mother. I had seen her sobbing when Jet died, and I had seen her unhappy countless times, wounded on her own or on someone else's behalf.

From my side of the bed, I said, "I made you cry once."

"You did," she agreed, and her musing, rather tender expression did not change.

Still musing and by way of explanation, she said simply, "Someone sets the tone in a house."

Someone sets the tone. The words sank in and have never left me.

LIVING ON SCRAPS

I MADE MY MOTHER CRY when we were at the lake, about twenty-five years ago. A lifetime led up to it, my lifetime and also hers.

We used to gather there in the last week of August, my parents, siblings, Mark and I, our children, Sochi and Ben. A semi-wilderness lake in eastern Ontario, not far from the Ottawa Valley, where my mother was born. My parents secured their waterfront lot in 1969 and had a small cabin built that consisted of one basic room with three sleeping cubicles, a rudimentary sink and shelves, a table, a woodstove and a screened-in porch. It sat in deep shade under trees my parents refused to cut back. We used an outdoor privy. We carried buckets of water up the steep slope from the little wooden dock. My parents slept on a set of bunks in one of the sleeping cubicles while the rest of us occupied the other two sets of bunks or retreated to tents outside.

Since it took seven hours to drive there from London, my parents generally went only twice a year, staying a week each time, in early May, before the bugs arrived, and again in late August after the bugs were gone. In the beginning I found the place dark and claustrophobic and avoided it like the plague, since it gave me my parents in undiluted form. I wasn't unlike the tender young tomato plants that keeled over when my mother, in open warfare with the marauding rabbits in her garden, had my father save his urine in a plastic jug and then poured it along the perimeter of the tomato row, staking out her territory. His urine was testosterone-rich and the colour of black tea, that being all he ever drank; he abhorred water and never let it pass his lips. The next day she looked out the kitchen window and every single tomato lay flat, dead as a doornail.

My opinion of the cabin softened when I introduced Mark to the lake in the summer of 1987 and his New York eyes fell in love with the trees, the canoes, the quiet. Even so, the place was guaranteed to churn me up. For instance, the summer before I made my mother cry we had gathered as usual in late August. For the first two days we all got along, but on the third day my mother and I locked horns and after that we could not look at each other. She got into a canoe and paddled one way and I got into another canoe and paddled the other way—something that invariably happened on day three at the cabin: canoes scattered in all directions.

A day or so later, after she and my father had departed for London and the others had left too, I was alone with the left-over food and the six-quart basket of rotting peaches from the tree in their garden—unsprayed, un-refrigerated, they rotted while you looked at them. I took the basket outside and proceeded to cut away the large bruises that formed in minutes, spread in seconds, one bruise producing another, two peaches curled around their mutual rotting—and I threw their soft, brown, mouldy parts into the woods, where they landed with a rustle. I threw the pits after them. I emptied out the entire basket humming with fruit flies, wild fruit and bruises as I sat under a dark sky, puffy and low, and pondered writing a letter to my mother about our latest scrap.

She had mildly criticized a relative for always finding fault with her small son. "My mother treated me like that," she said. "I understand the boy's moodiness." When I defended the woman, she said, enunciating each word, "I don't want to get into an argument about this with you."

"It's only an argument if you make it one," I said in turn.

The woods were full of bruises by the time I finished. Afterwards, I went back into the cabin and gobbled food without restraint, stuffing my face with everything she had saved and set aside for me: the last serving of steak and kidney pudding, the pea soup, the bacon, the preserves, the cashews. Then I washed the dishes in lots of soapy water instead of the evil grey two inches she allowed in the dishpan.

I went to bed that night thinking "good and bad, and sometimes they were very sad."

A few weeks after my slaughter of the peaches, her letter arrived in the mail. I read it and thought: I'm insane. A letter so affectionate, so typical of all her letters, it was as if nothing untoward had happened between us. I felt enormous relief and also astonishment. In her mind had nothing happened? But of course this was her way of dealing with what had happened. She wanted to forget it, wanted me to forget it. Her letter was a peace offering and these were the conditions of peace: that we not discuss it. In her gentle way she was reading me the riot act.

Not only that, though. She was telling me she loved me. And reading the letter, I felt loved.

It opened with the quotation she was planning to use on her Arctic diptych of Lancaster Sound, two big paintings inspired by the memorial on Beechey Island to Franklin and his ill-fated expedition. *In those Northwest Voyages where navigation must be executed in most exquisite sort. John Davis, 1594.*

I suspect she was working away in her studio when the diptych cohered in her mind thanks to those words. And thanks to those words, she felt able to write to me from an unobstructed heart. In those Northwest Voyages through a difficult family where navigation must be executed in most exquisite sort.

When I was in my twenties my mother and I went for a walk across the fields that bordered their home, and found treasure of a sort. We had taken the road leading through a gully and were on our way past a big new home, recently built, when she spied a waterfall of onions spilling down the grassy bank into a shallow ravine. "Onions!" she said. "We'll come back for those."

I suggested they might be there for a reason, maybe the people in that house meant them to be there.

"Oh, no. They've been thrown out. Imagine anyone throwing out onions."

"Maybe they're bad."

"No." She knelt down and palmed one, pressing her finger through the mush into "good firm onion." Then stood up and set off again, as though renewed.

Saving excited her. To find onions and return with several bags in the evening when fewer people might see, then carry them home to cut away the bad parts and add the remainder to a casserole, then eat them, then taste them for hours afterwards. At the time I was reading Gertrude Stein, so I was familiar with her observation that the French find it interesting to save and dull to spend, a thought so pertinent and beguiling I noted it down for later use. When Gertrude's dog died, a poodle named Basket, Picasso advised her never to get the same kind of dog again. Being Gertrude she got the same kind of dog and gave it the same name. Her love of continuity, which she said she learned from the French—*le roi est mort, vive le roi*—outweighed Picasso's love of endings.

Even for the French, I rather think, those onions would have been considered past saving. My mother, however, guarded them as she would an orphan in a storm.

She used every last morsel of every last morsel, her kitchen full of tiny properties, tiny brushstrokes of food that she controlled like an impressionist painter. She knew where every jot of food was at whatever distance, so that what looked like a blur to anyone else's eyes was a landscape to hers. If you ate something, she knew. She knew the heft of every cut of meat, the shape of every piece of cheese, the number of cookies in every tin.

Making me a cup of tea during one of my visits home—by this time I might have been in my thirties—she removed the teabag after it barely touched the water, then put it aside to be reused, and I had to say, "Don't you think I'm capable of deciding when to fish out the teabag?"

A cool silence after that.

The thermostat was out of bounds. I wrapped myself in sweaters. She put her faded pink thick woollen bathrobe on over her clothes and worked all morning in her nearly unheated studio, painting a canvas as she painted her toast, controlling each stroke. I recall opening her fridge and seeing on the butter dish a stroke of butter, no bigger than a clipped fingernail, where it was being saved for an occasion worthy of butter.

The phrase came to me during that visit: living on scraps. The life that animates old anger and feeds on it, making yet another meal from sorry bits and pieces of the past, and letting nothing go.

The summer after the peaches, and once again at the lake, I saw her sitting all by herself, leaning her back against the cement block that we used as an anchor when we went fishing. It was almost suppertime, but there she was beside the water instead of near the woodstove.

Earlier she had accused me of throwing chicken juices down the drain. "When we came for dinner a year ago," she said. Her bald, matter-of-fact words followed some brief discussion about suet. My sister-in-law had made the tourtière pastry from suet and lard, half and half, and my mother expressed surprise; she never used suet anymore. Like everyone else she was on the health bandwagon, so now she made her steamed puddings with margarine. "You're the same," she said to me.

"Oh no, I don't hold with any of that." Breezily refusing to go along with her. "Suet, butter, lard—a little of any of it is okay."

"Then why did you throw those perfectly good chicken juices and fat down the sink last year?"

I stopped in my tracks. *What was she talking about?* "I didn't. I never throw out chicken juices. I use them in soup."

"You did, you threw them out. And I think I was noble to have held my tongue."

Her jocular tone did not mean she wasn't serious.

"A year ago!" I protested. "A year ago!" And I appealed to the room in general and Mark in particular, since by this time he was the only other person in the cabin. "You've been holding on to this for a year?"

"And I think I was noble to have held my tongue," she repeated, her face bright, lively. She must have been doing something with her hands, she always was, and what was I doing? Standing there, feeling attacked, since nothing mattered more to my mother than wasted food. I went into one of the sleeping cubicles to put on my swimsuit and when I came out, I strode over to the kitchen shelf, rapped the cookie tin with my hand and quoted the motto that ran around its side: "'When I do ill, I hear it ever.'" (There were four sides to the tin, and the motto in its Scottish entirety ran: "When I do well, I hear it never, when I do ill, I hear it ever.") And now she was shocked. "Oh, Lizzie. I was just teasing you."

She was only a foot away from me, her face tanned, expressive (was she brushing her hair?).

"You're a hard person to cook for," I said deliberately.

"Why?" She was bewildered. How could I say such a thing of her?

"I bring food and you tell me to take it home, there's too much food, take it home."

"Lizzie. That's because there are four of you and two of us. We can't possibly eat it all."

"Well," I said again, "all I can say is, you're a hard person to cook for."

"I'm sorry. I don't mean to be."

And what was I really saying? What I had wanted to say for days, ever since I had begun to prepare for this short spell together at the lake. A week of arguments in my head (laid end to end they would encircle the globe), during which I had imagined her paving the way for me by repeating, as she never tired of repeating, that your father is wonderful to cook for, I cook and he eats and he never, ever complains. "Well, you're not wonderful to cook for," I had been itching to say, thinking of the time she told Dad's secretary that she was going to send her our dental bills if she kept bringing us candy-festooned cakes, and the time she told the toothy home economics teacher that she must have made the cookies with coconut because Mr. Hay hated coconut, and the times she had told me to take home the food I had put considerable effort into making for these bloody, fucked-up family gatherings.

If I told her I would bring a meal: "Don't, we always have too much."

Or if I brought the food: "Take it home, we have too much already."

If we brought fresh bagels, she would have old bagels that had to be eaten. "Take yours home. Take them back."

We had to eat her food first. "We *have* to," she would invariably say, "or it will go bad. Take yours home."

Only her food mattered, her poor, sad, lonely scraps that nobody wanted to eat.

When I think of what I was forced to swallow as a child! Watery baked custard made worse by the wretched skin on top; slimy porridge, lumpy, grey, going cold; loose and soggy bread pudding with raisins as distended as the bellies of the muskrats Jet brought home and left in the yard to swell up in the hot sun; sausages so greasy they clogged my throat and brought tears to my eyes; mashed turnip so fibrous and stringy I had to sieve it through my teeth; soup made from beef bones with globules of fat floating on top; even, from time to time, tongue, which meant the cow's raspy taste buds met mine; and tapioca, another calamity of awful textures.

No mercy, no mercy. "Eat it, I don't care whether you choke," she would say. And my father never failed to back her up. "Elizabeth," removing his wristwatch, his lower lip dangerously atremble, "you have two minutes to finish your turnip."

My sister says the soundtrack to every meal was the scraping of my spoon against my teeth.

I went for my swim and found that I was almost shaking. Mark said, "She apologized. Let it go."

We paddled to the raft, had our swim, paddled back. As we were tying up the canoe to the overhanging cedar, she came down to the water looking around for the pile of wood my father had sawed into woodstove-lengths, but it wasn't there because I had carried it up earlier. She said to herself, "It's gone," then wandered, looking a bit lost, over to the short, tilting dock on the far side of the cedars. Sitting down, she rested her back against the cement block and stared out at the water, a little figure in brown and maroon, her maroon pants some synthetic material widened by a band of nearly matching fabric running from ankle to waist on each leg (she had let out and refashioned my father's pants in the same way), plus an old brown blouse softened with age, her arms bare, her head from the back that beautiful silvery-white. It was after five o'clock, yet she wasn't at the stove.

I wrapped a towel around my middle as Mark went up the path to the cabin, and I went over to her. She didn't turn but continued to stare at the water. I leaned down and kissed the side of her head. "I love you, Mom."

She looked up. "So that's good, then." Her face was all broken up and tormented and I said to myself, She is really, really upset. I sank down beside her—she was facing the water and I was facing her and the woods behind and the cabin high in the woods. I said, "I'm sorry I hurt you, but I felt so criticized."

She said, "How can you feel that way? I just don't understand. We think you're wonderful. We don't feel *any* criticism toward you. None." Tears were streaming down her face. "I thought we were all getting along so well. Everybody's been wonderful." And she listed everyone's names, my husband, my brother, my sister-in-law, my kids.

"So that gives us the chance not to be," I laughed.

But she wasn't ready for laughter. "How can you say you feel criticized? We have nothing but admiration for what you're doing. Your dad and I. We're just so *proud.*" Her tears were so thick she choked on the word and clenched her hands in impatience—annoyance—at her lack of control. "So *proud,*" she managed to get out again, her lips and lower jaw shaking uncontrollably, "so proud of everything you're doing."

I believed her, up to a point. "You touched a tender spot," I said, "this one of food." Did she think I didn't know that in her eyes wasting food was the crime of crimes? "I don't remember anything about chicken juices a year ago."

"Lizzie, I was only teasing you. So I guess I can't joke with you." She was defensive, stiff, accusing.

"You're not being fair to me," I said.

"I know. I should grow up. I should just grow up."

By then, or perhaps at that moment, I put my arms around her, this woman not much bigger than my daughter, her skin as warm and smooth, deeply sorry for having made her cry, yet in my head I couldn't help thinking, What about the cutting things you said on the telephone? The harsh looks directed at my son? What about the book I wrote that you buried? What about the letter you wrote saying you wouldn't let Dad read it? How could you be so repelled by my book, and the "*bleak*" person it revealed me to be, that you deep-sixed the damn thing, yet still tell me you're "nothing but proud"? And even as I held her in my arms and mopped her face with my T-shirt, even as I felt shamefaced at having

28

settled the score with her and wondered which of us was the more childish (but hurt has no age), I still felt exasperated by her wilful blindness. If that's what it was.

"I *feel* criticized," I said.

"*I* feel so criticized," she said. "How can *you* feel criticized? We never say *anything*."

"I know what's going on in your head, I know what you're thinking." Then in a different tone, "And I know how critical I am too."

"You mean what you *think* I'm thinking." And she wailed, "I want to go home. I want to be in my studio where nobody bothers me."

She was weeping still. "I don't know what's the matter. Well, your father got into a snit. I don't know why. Well, he's—" She stopped herself. Then, "He can't work with anybody. I asked him to put some wood on the fire and when I moved one of the sticks he flew off the handle."

I was still holding her in my arms. The word in my mind, though it took a while to surface, was "tenderize." I was thinking about what you do to tough meat before cooking it: you pound it with a mallet to make the cramped muscle give way. You feel yourself yield and make room for a fuller picture of someone else. Her words had stung me, mine had stung her back, and now we were giving way to each other.

"You'll want to wear this," she said, handing my T-shirt back to me and reaching for the corner of her blouse. But there were more tears. I gave her my T-shirt again. Then before we went up the path, "Wait," I said. I wet the end of my shirt in the lake and gave it to her to wash her eyes, which were puffy and red, though she didn't seem to care. I suppose I cared. I didn't want others to see that I had made my mother cry.

———

For the next two days everything was peaceful. In the morning, while light rain fell outside, I raised her hand-held slide viewer (mended with Scotch tape) up to the window and looked at slides of her recent paintings. I saw lichens as they appeared under her microscope, the longitudinal section of a thallus and the cuplike fruiting bodies: images that in her paintings came to resemble oriental script. Her great subject now that she was in her seventies had become the vastness of the High Arctic and its minute and delicate plant life.

She had made her first of several trips to Ellesmere Island when she was in her late sixties, living among scientists in their tents, exploring, photographing, planning her large-scale paintings and having the time of her life. Those were the days in Canada, and they were brief, when something called the Arctic Awareness Program funded visual artists to travel to scientific camps in the Far North, thus providing an artistic complement to scientific work, and vice versa.

Much of her work was large scale, but she also made small Arctic assemblages from pocket-sized things she had picked up on her northern travels: the feather of a snow bunting, a preserved wood chip from Axel Heiberg Island, Arctic poppy seedpods, the twiglike branch of an Arctic willow, a ptarmigan feather, stones and shells from Beechey Island, the mandible of an Arctic hare, a small piece of an olivine stone found at the base of a glacier. These she arranged and mounted on sheets of thick paper that she had made by hand by gathering plants, boiling them, beating them with bits of cotton or linen or silk and pressing them to remove the excess water, so that when you looked at the result you were seeing, among other transformed things, the seedpods of milkweed, a wasp's nest, cattail roots, birch bark, wheat chaff, the yucca plant from her garden and burdock from the fields.

Poetry and oppression, that's what living with my mother was like. She opened a plastic bag and showed me three silk-worm cocoons—ivory, skinlike, a few strands of dangling silk—collected on the trip to China they had taken in the spring. She dropped one of the cocoons into a cup of water while I watched, and stirred with her finger, then lifted out the cocoon and pulled on threads that came loose and trailed out, long, incredibly strong. She hadn't yet decided how she would use them, but she would find a way.

Since my mother saved scrap paper for me, bringing loose reams of it whenever we got together, every so often I would turn over a page offhandedly at my desk and see my father's long, loping handwriting, stunned at how similar it was to mine. Sometimes I turned over a page and met my mother. *Rodman Hall. Arts Centre. Dear Jean Hay, I am sorry to relate that none of your works were selected for this year's exhibition.* I had been writing on the back of her disappointment. Even rejection she saved.

In the short memoir she wrote in her early eighties while she was waiting long months for the operation to replace her hip, she recalled being six years old in primer class in Renfrew, Ontario. Christmas was approaching, and Miss Clemens, her redheaded teacher, asked everyone to make a Christmas drawing. *I drew a Christmas tree. It was magnificent. Then I tackled a star, five-pointed, at the top—the final flourish. Unsuccessful. Tried again. And again. And again, rubbing out in succession each botched attempt, and ending up with a hole in the cheap paper where the star should have been and tears dripping onto the drawing. At which point,*

Miss Clemens produced, not a red, or blue, or even silver star but a Gold star to cover the hole.

A year later another gaping hole opened up in front of her eyes, but this one nothing could ever fill. *In the spring of the year when I was seven, my much-loved father died and my world never recovered. There is a vivid picture I'll carry in my mind—my father comatose in bed, the spring breezes lifting the curtains of the open window, bird songs from outside and that semi-circle of solid dark Stevenson bodies sitting silent, waiting for him to die. It was too much. I started to cry. . . . Yet memories of him abound—little incidents. He carrying me to the blueberry patch, sitting me down under bushes where I picked and ate my own berries; carrying me to the front of the Sunday school Christmas pageant to recite my little piece: scared mute, I clung to him and couldn't be coaxed to open my mouth; eating supper with my high chair beside him and holding his hand; then to bed, up the stairs piggyback (this is the one memory of my mother that has stuck) while mother came behind tickling, none too gently. I laughed and shrieked anyway. Somersaults on the big bed, and, without fail, as he got to the landing on the stairs, calling out from my crib, "Daddy, I need a drink of water." And back he would come.*

About eight years later, when Vilhjalmur Stefansson, the famous Arctic explorer, came through the Ottawa Valley on the Chautauqua lecture circuit, she heard him speak and saw his slides of Arctic flowers whose beauty she would remember until her dying day. *I must have known it was everything I'd been looking for,* she wrote after finally seeing the Far North with her own eyes. *The silence, the clarity of the air, the startling purity of the colours, the beginnings of flora—lichens, grasses, mosses—as though the world was, once again, new.*

———

It's curious the way anger dissipates. Like opening an orange. The segments come apart, there's broken flesh and too much juice, and it's simply easier to wash your hands. I have to work, right now, to remember what kept me awake so many nights. The more I write, the more benign my parents seem.

I remember a trip my mother and I made to New York City to visit art galleries when I was twenty-eight and she was sixty. She was the best companion in a gallery, full of insights and candour. In front of Goya's *The Forge*, she explained the composition: a series of diagonals around the red circle of fire. In front of an Ad Reinhardt: all the hues contained in what at first glance was nothing but black. "It's a revelation to see the colours emerge," she said. Of a lesser Degas: "He wasn't *always* good." And her voice was full of satisfaction. "Look." She pointed to the traces of blue under a white sky in a work by Milton Avery. "He changed his mind." And when I asked her how she knew, maybe he had that in mind all along, she simply grinned and said, "I'm looking for the struggle."

She had packed food for the trip, so at midday we searched out a bench in Central Park and she opened her shoulder bag and handed me pieces of cheese, homemade oatcakes, celery. It was February. My fingers turned blue around the celery. "Put on your gloves," she said, amused and inflexible. I did not rebel until our last day, when I told her I was going into that café over there to buy myself a cup of coffee. "Really?" We sat at the counter and I ordered coffee while she drank a glass of water.

She had no need for such creature comforts; she had no need to spend. What Gertrude Stein said: she found spending dull. It offended her sense of ingenuity and thrift.

In those days she was painting veiled women. She and my father had made a trip to Morocco in 1978 to visit my oldest brother, Stu, who was teaching there. They travelled across North Africa, and in Algeria she raised her camera to snap a picture of a burka-clad woman in a doorway. The woman turned her back and faced the door. My mother took a picture of that. Once she got home, she pulled a nylon stocking over her face to feel what it was like to be rendered so aggressively invisible and she painted a portrait of her features pressed flat. Then she went on to do a series of big canvases of veiled women in doorways.

Grim subject matter occupied her for a long time. The feathers of a caged golden eagle; animals in traps; wounded hands. There was her poignant explanation a few days before my first wedding, when I was thirty and she was still in her sixties, of a series of drawings she was doing about ambiva-lence. She had wanted to use her engagement ring as the image, she told me, but thought that would be too painful for "your dad." She used her amethyst brooch instead, a jewel held in place by tiny gold claws. On the eve of my wedding she was gently telling me something drastic about marriage. About what I was getting myself into, about going on anyway, about continuity. *Le roi est mort, vive le roi.*

And now I'm remembering another visit home when I was in my thirties. Perhaps I've written these pages in order to arrive here again. It was summer. We were in her bright, sunlit kitchen, standing side by side at the counter, slicing fruit and arranging the slices around mounds of cottage cheese on plates we then carried outside into the shade of the apple tree. The plates were flowered and old and un-matching. I sat in a folding chair near my mother and drank in the satin sheen of her brown arms, the glint of her silver hair, her girlish slenderness. She was seventy and could have passed for fifty-five.

I have never known another person to chew her food so thoroughly. The more she chewed, the longer the food lasted and the more it nourished her. I feel sure that's how her thinking went. She was getting her money's worth, making the most of every bite. It was her invariable practice to have a negligible breakfast followed by a small lunch, then a sizable dinner, after which she enjoyed satiation like an Eskimo of old after a long fast. I asked her once why she didn't eat more during the day and less at night, but my chiding missed the point. The point was the self-imposed drama of her eating, the daylong discipline and then the release.

Now when I think of eating with her, I think of this: outside, without a table, the food in her lap cradled like a child.

THEIR DEPARTURE

"SOMEONE SETS THE TONE," my mother said from her bed in the spare room. And listening to her talk, keeping her company, I appreciated for the first time the counterweight she consciously tried to provide to my father's irascible gloom. Around the same time she said something else, something so striking I wrote it down and used it in the novel I was working on. "The older you get," she said, "the closer your loves are to the surface."

One unfinished painting was now pressing on her mind more than any other: the portrait of my brother Al. She had painted all of her children when we were small: Stu holding a precious stuffed animal in his arms; second-born Al with a huge fixed grin on his face; me sitting on a stool with my head bowed over a book; my younger sister when she was three or four, her round face so bewitching we thought her the most beautiful child in the history of the world.

The portrait of Al my mother later destroyed, believing it did not do him justice, and now she urgently wanted to redress the imbalance. Her plan was to base the new picture on a black-and-white snapshot of him fishing amid a cloud of flies when he was three years old. *Young Al Fishing*, she called it. The unfolding drama of this image—its loss, its rediscovery, its various beleaguered manifestations—would be the creative thread that ran to the end of her days.

———

In early December, the infection in her knee roared back. She underwent a second operation, once again under full anaesthetic, and after that her mind was never the same.

I recall an afternoon close to Christmas. She had been home for a week after this second operation, and the long-anticipated visit by the gallery curator was soon to happen, if not this month then next. We took paintings off the walls and brought others in from the studio and carried them to where she sat on the chesterfield with a big felt pen in her hand. She had always signed her name on the back of her canvases: Jean Hay.

First, she had to practise writing her name on an envelope. It took a few stabs for her to get the hang of it. She signed the first canvas. Then she attempted to write its title beside her name. "How do you spell lichen?" she asked, and I saw that she had made a start and written *lik*. On the next canvas she got partway through "abandoned" and needed help. She even got stuck on "of," spelling it *ov*. She was unsure how to write 2008. All her sawmill paintings were painted in 2008, we knew that with certainty, and other dates we guessed at. The state of her mind was very much in tune with the state of her knee, and with the sawmill paintings themselves, since the enormous incision looked like the teeth of a saw.

A day or so later, for the whole of an afternoon, her mind miraculously returned to itself. She had invited two friends to come by and choose for themselves either a painting or a drawing to keep. Before they arrived, she sat with a clipboard in her lap, assembling her thoughts about each work on offer and writing them down on scrap paper. This is what she wrote without apparent effort and only the odd mistake in spelling:

1. mysterious hills and icebergs. Greely Fiord hills formed when techtonic plates shift to allow eruptions of hot lava to boil up and eject former sedimentary ocean layered bottom to rear upwards to form striated hills. Icebergs softened by light snowfall.

2. Part of snout of Greely Glacier reflected in the fiord—snout is 2½ miles across. Fiord empties into saltwater ocean east of Ellesmere Island.

3. Arctic lichen growing on rocks ? yrs. Growing in non-polluted air and trampled seldom by muskox.

4. Greely Fiord hills and bergs. Fiord can be crossed at low tide on foot. It too is 2+ miles across. I am standing on south side of fiord looking north (I think) and assessing the cold threat of that obscure in a way menacing fog. Hidden shore opposite.

5. The idea behind the two drawings of hands was of compassion and healing. A friend who sprained his wrist invited me to observe the warm-wax treatment and the result was not only drawings but also paintings.

The next day, the tent pegs of her memory pulled out again and her mind was like Yeats's "tattered coat upon a stick."

Christmas week that year, 2008, was full of snow squalls followed by a week of high winds. In early January her leg ballooned and fluid gathered in her lungs: congestive heart failure. But she hung on. There were more trips to the clinic, more tests, more storminess from my father as we tried to figure out the logistics of the move to Ottawa and the sale of the house.

In the midst of this chaos, the curator arrived. She proved to be a large, hearty woman of middle age wearing a straight skirt and an electric-blue top. She came into the living room rather like a tractor and handled the situation as a tractor would have, riding over my tiny mother with outsized good humour. All too quickly it became clear that she had no interest in my mother's most recent work. She had her eye instead on the painting my mother had offered to donate, an early work not by her but by a young artist friend who had since become famous.

My mother sat beside the curator on the chesterfield, all genial courtesy as her mind shifted in and out of focus. "We've lived in this house since the war," she said. "Did you do elementary school here?" she asked me with a smile. I gently amended—no, that was in Wiarton and Mitchell— and was relieved when she didn't appear to be flustered by the yawning gap in her sense of time. She kept making pleasant conversation and so did the curator.

After the visit was over and the curator had gone, my mother said not a word about the fate of her paintings. She carried on as if nothing untoward had happened, as if she had not pinned a year's worth of effort and hope on this visit, and she never mentioned the curator again.

Neither did I. I was not about to disturb her equanimity by probing to see what it amounted to. Had forgetfulness come to her rescue, or pride? Or some new acceptance that the fate of her final paintings didn't really matter anymore?

At every meal she emptied her little woven basket of pills onto the table and made compositions with them, like

Cézanne arranging his peaches. She was too weak and crippled to venture into her studio, a trip that entailed going out the kitchen door into the sun porch and across the porch to the stairwell landing with its view of the studio just below, reached by a flight of steps that turned rather sharply at the bottom. Then one afternoon in the middle of January, when no one was looking, she headed out there by herself. She ditched her walker in the sun porch, switched to her cane and was about to descend the stairs unaided when I saw what she was up to and caught up with her and took her arm. I helped her down the stairs—nothing would dissuade her—and stayed with her as she put on the oversized down jacket she had taken to wearing in the studio to keep herself warm. She perched herself on a stool and proceeded to go through tubes of paint and jars of paintbrushes. She was separating out which supplies she would take with her to Ottawa and which she would donate to an amateur painting group.

Setting aside some of the paintbrushes but pulling most of them toward her, she said, "I want to be generous but not *too* generous."

Then, "This is like giving my life's blood!"

I watched her and felt as if I were watching my last sunset.

The previous summer I had helped her cook the surface of what turned out to be her last big painting, four feet by five, a study of the delicate grey-and-white pattern in a stone she had picked up at Lake Tuborg on Ellesmere Island. The painting lay flat on the big, long table in her studio awaiting the final stage of the encaustic method she had been using for twenty years or more. Together we brushed its surface with warm beeswax medium, she taking one paintbrush, I the other. The liquid medium went waxy as soon as it touched the cool canvas, and we bent close and cocked our heads to make sure we left no patches bare. Then she showed me how to circle the heat lamp slowly over a small area. "I count to eight," she said, before moving on to the next area, cooking every inch of canvas. Under the warmth of the lamp the medium melted and pooled and our brushstrokes disappeared. The result was a delicate surface sheen that completed the painting and protected it.

The grey-and-white stone was one of three she had picked up from the bed of a creek that flowed into the glacially fed, virtually inaccessible lake. The scientists my mother was camping with told her the stones were four and a half million years old, and hers were the first pair of eyes to see them. Adding to her sense of the extraordinary was what happened next. A week after she got home, that part of the creek bed, and all of the instruments measuring its water levels, were swept away when the face of the glacier sheared off and a flood of ice, stones, water and debris buried everything in their path. In picking up and pocketing the stones, she had rescued them from oblivion. They were her Ishmael, if you like.

In her painting memoir she marvelled at how something that otherwise would have been lost from view for an eternity had come into her possession, a girl from the Ottawa Valley. "I can't believe that the person I see climbing a hill in the Arctic is *me*," she had written. "It's vaguely like me but not really me. It *can't* be me. Yet it *is* me."

On that same January day when she was sorting through her art supplies, the family from across the street came over to see the house. Stu had taken on the job of selling it (meanwhile Al was looking for homes for my mother's art, contacting galleries that already had some of her work; anything they did not want, we children would keep). These neighbours, who made an offer within half an hour of their visit, asked my father how he was. He had been standing to the side, considering them as they admired the living room.

"*Rotten*," he said, and swung away from them and headed down the hall. Then more resignedly, throwing it over his shoulder, "But all right."

My parents left their beloved home on January 24th, 2009. The frenzied lead-up to their departure reminded me of the flight into Egypt, except that Mary had misplaced her son and was desperate to find him.

While we filled a few suitcases to take on the small plane to Ottawa, while Stu scheduled the moving truck and sorted belongings, while my mother's knee remained "nice and quiet," according to the surgeon, thus allowing her to travel—while all this was going on, she searched obsessively for two things: the slide she'd had made of the small black-and-white snapshot from 1952 of young Al fishing, and the enlargement made from the slide.

"Where might they be?" I asked my father. "Have you seen them?"

"In her head," was his answer.

On the eve of our departure, I went out into her studio to make another search and paused for a moment to take stock of everything and appreciate it for the last time: the huge canvases leaning against walls and stacked on shelves; the oversized easel; the big canvas-covered, paint-bespattered table, one end of which was covered with a sheet of glass; the several stained lab coats, hanging from a hook by the small sink, that she wore over her clothes while she worked; the many tubes of paint in margarine tubs; the puddles of paint in the hollows of muffin tins. I took in the enormity of the enterprise. My mother had kept it up, this mighty effort, for over forty years. "I don't think anybody has worked harder," my sister said to me once. And not for money either. From the show that marked her eightieth birthday, a show that sold well, she earned $700 after expenses. The gallery owner charged her for the framing and half the cost of the flyers, and took half the price of every painting sold. Three years of work, she said to me.

It was a cold day, and that night the temperature dropped even lower. We got ourselves to bed, my mother in the spare room, me in the adjoining one, my father across the hall, Stu downstairs in the study. (Stu would drive the three of us to the airport the next afternoon, then return to the house and begin the job of emptying it.) After midnight, noises from the kitchen woke me, and I went out to discover my hungry mother on the prowl for non-existent rhubarb and salmon. Soon my father joined us, and in our pyjamas we had a Horlicks picnic, drinking the hot, soothing malted drink and eating cookies.

We sat on mismatched stools at the wide island of a countertop, my father on the tall wooden stool, me on the metal folding stool, my mother on the seat of her walker. The kitchen was steeped in hard work, frugality, prosperity, memories. Over the years, as the family grew in size, each grandchild's face was added to the rogues' gallery of snapshots on either side of the door leading into the dining room, until the walls were blanketed with the past and future.

Over his Horlicks my father confessed to an episode he said would follow him to the grave: he had failed to pay a parking fine incurred at the hospital. "So we *have* to leave town," he said, giving us a good laugh.

I said, "Tomorrow Mark will be waiting for us at the airport with open arms."

My mother said, "I borrow his arms first."

We put our mugs beside the sink and went back to bed and for a while we slept. Before dawn sounds from the kitchen woke me again, and I went out to find my mother on her walker, heading toward the back door.

"I'm just heading out to find that photo of Al," she said over her shoulder.

She was in her nightgown, a sweater thrown over her shoulders, tiny, stooped, hell-bent.

"Mom, we looked yesterday and the day before, and it's not there." I took her hands and kissed and wept and laughed into them. I dissuaded her, convinced that the photo existed in the same deluded world as the salmon and rhubarb.

All that morning we toiled away. At lunch we sat at the dining room table, the last occasion we were ever to do so. Then early in the afternoon, an hour and a half before we were to leave for the airport, I was startled to see on the kitchen counter a lone photographic slide, and paper-clipped to one corner, a slip of scrap paper that said "Young Al Fishing."

Stu, thorough and undramatic, had found it in the hand-held slide viewer in the studio, the one mended with Scotch tape, a place I had never thought to look.

Holding it up to the kitchen window, I saw my brother Al with his famous fishing pole extended over the water. There *was* a slide, after all.

Now—finally heeding my mother—I helped her down the stairs to her studio once again, where she darted this way and that on her cane, sorting through paintings, far more organized in her mind than I had given her credit for being.

"Ah, I don't know. I don't know," she said. "I want to *finish* that. That is a must. Then the three with the abandoned church—or house—the hill that goes up beside the tree. It's going to be called 'Abandoned. St. Kilda.' Now where is the— That's number one and two of the sawmill, and that's three, unfinished. And that's St. Kilda. I've got that drawing too. I wonder where it is. There it is, there it is. Let's get it out to the front. Then there's the other one. No. There it is. That's the fourth one. And five is our little guy. Those are the five I want to get finished."

She stood still. "I don't know how I'll do it where I'll be living."

I stood beside her in the full knowledge that she never would. In Ottawa they would have a one-bedroom suite with space for nothing more than a small worktable. I didn't say anything and neither did she. On our left the big windows were dotted here and there with coloured decals to divert songbirds away from the glass. Winter light poured in and sifted over everything.

We continued to circle the studio and all the while I kept my eye out for the enlargement made from the slide. Almost by chance—though how had I not looked there before?—I found myself at the bulletin board above the sink where she washed her brushes. She had pinned up various clippings over the years, including assorted directions to herself and a slip of paper with the handwritten words *beautiful, mysterious and full of meaning*. These six words went all the way back to New York City and the woman who walked over to my mother's work on the wall of our apartment on West 105th and made that ecstatic pronouncement. I had passed on the compliment and she had jotted it down and pinned it here. A large unmarked white envelope was thumb-tacked to the board. I took it down and opened it. There was the enlargement of Al.

"Mom!"

I showed it to her, and she said, "*There* it is."

A triumph amid the ruins. (And what a ruins. Her workshop, her art, her life's blood, all left behind.)

An hour later, we were backing down the sloping driveway. Stu was behind the wheel, my father beside him. My mother and I were in the back seat. After we turned onto the snowy street, Stu looked back at the house. We all did—all except my mother, whose lively glance was fixed on the road ahead. Then my brother drove on. The road curved up a hill and out to a cross street. We turned left and headed toward the airport and away from a neighbourhood they would never see again.

My father turned around in his seat and said to my mother, his voice hurt and full of reproach, "You didn't even look back."

She smiled a little and nodded, utterly free of remorse, it seemed. There were other things on her mind. Maybe this is what my father meant when he said he had never seen her unhappy. Maybe he meant that in comparison to *him* she was never unhappy.

We flew to Ottawa on one of those tiny planes that seats a dozen people. It took about fifty minutes, a bumpy flight, the three of us buckled into our seats, my father stoical, my mother, as always, game for anything.

It was dark when we landed. Snow flew about in the blasting January wind. Attendants came. One of them lifted my mother in his arms and carried her down the stairs, then put her into a wheelchair and pushed her across the tarmac. My father and I followed close behind, Dad unsteady on his feet, both of us blown about. We could have been in a reader's dream of Russia, so desolate was the snowy wasteland all around us. But there, in the brightly lit area as we came through the glass door, was Mark with his open arms.

HIS TEMPER

OVER THE YEARS, whenever I thought of asking my mother about my father's temper, this is what I wanted to happen. I wanted her to go still and thoughtful, closer to herself and closer to me. I wanted us to be sitting outside, maybe looking at the clothes drying on the line, garments and linens flapping in a summer breeze. I wanted her face to soften and her eyes to turn inward, back to that day long ago when she discovered she had married a man with a violent temper. And even though over the course of their long marriage she had always hidden behind the usual devices, saying he didn't mean it, he regretted it, he was a deeply good man, far better than she—didn't he always return to the newspaper box and add more coins if he had put in less than the right amount of change?—I wanted her to let all excuses slide away and take me back to the moment that must have shocked her to the core of her being, for she was someone who could not bear emotional conflict of any kind. When did you first see Dad lose his temper? What happened next? What did it cost you? And I would sit and listen, and remember every turn of phrase and change in expression on my mother's face.

My first memory of his temper is not my first memory of being punished. They are distinct, the latter slow and calculated and having to do with tulips, and the former an explosion at the dining room table with consequences that lasted for hours. After I picked those fetching red tulips in the Cheethams' garden across the street in Owen Sound, I was sent upstairs to my room to wait for him to come home. I would have been about three years old. It was a long wait, lying on my bed in the brightness of the afternoon, listening for his step on the stairs and his hand on the doorknob. He entered and without looking especially angry, without looking angry at all, came over to the bed and methodically spanked me. This was the only case of delayed punishment I can remember. No, there was another.

Several years later, after we had moved farther up the Bruce Peninsula to Wiarton, I was walking up the street one summer's day with a friend, sucking on a forbidden lollipop, when my father drove by. He saw me and I saw him, and I shoved my lollipop into my friend's hand as he pulled over to the curb. We were not allowed to buy candy: it was an iron rule for all his children. My father said not a word as I got in beside him. He drove to the end of the block and parked and went into the post office. My friend walked by, saw me in the car and jauntily waved the two lollipops, hers and mine, amazed at her good fortune. I looked away in great bitterness. My father came back with the mail, which he put on the seat between us, and we drove home. That meant the length of Berford Street, then up alarming Queen's Hill, a beautifully steep rise, almost death-defying, to Gould Street, then right on Gould past several houses to the smaller hill at the top of which our driveway poked off to the left. Somewhere on Berford Street, about where the *Wiarton Echo* had its building, he turned his stern face toward me and asked me what my middle name was. I told him. He replied with withering disgust, "Are you sure it isn't Sneak?" And I knew I was really in for it.

He pulled into our driveway and parked the car close to the house. I got out. He did not. A slow moment later, as I went around the back of the car and headed for the verandah, bracing myself, he got out too, and sure enough he came at me and walloped me on my way by. Frequently, his blows made me pee. Then there would be the humiliation of wet underpants, and if it happened inside, a puddle of urine on the floor.

My first memory of him exploding in fury goes back to the same era as the tulips, when I was about three years old. It was dinnertime and all five of us were at the dining room table (my sister not yet born). In memory the dining room in Owen Sound was rather dark despite the big bay window—dark wood trim, dark furniture, and directly below us, a sooty basement full of coal and a monster furnace. Al did something, he misbehaved in some way, and Dad sent him from the table, told him to go upstairs. But my brother moved too slowly. Dad surged from his chair and in one terrifying motion grabbed my brother with both hands and threw him. Al hit the steel radiator under the bay window and his head split open.

The doctor came. How quiet it was by that time and darker in a different way. No lights had been turned on. By then my brother was lying on his bed upstairs. I heard my parents in the hallway speaking in hushed, grateful voices to the doctor. They were thanking him for coming, saying goodbye. I was still at the dining room table, as I remember it. Still sitting with my supper in front of me. An accident, my mother said years later when I asked her about it. That was an accident.

Al would have been about five then. This brother would become in a few more years my father's favourite (along with my sister), a boy who could tease and be teased, a competitive, high-spirited, very smart boy who openly admired Dad and tried to emulate him—his walk, for instance, his long stride.

I asked Al recently what he remembered of that moment. We were sitting downstairs in my kitchen, reminiscing. He said he remembered coming to on the bathroom floor, Mom's face hovering over him, and hearing her say, "Oh, Gord!" My brother caught her stricken tone perfectly and she blossomed in front of me, the whole scene did.

I was twelve when my father's physical punishments ended in a final ignominious spill of urine as he dragged me by my hair across the kitchen floor. The blows stopped in time for puberty to clobber me.

One summer evening, before I had any children of my own, I took the train from Toronto to London to visit my parents and arrived to a thunderstorm in the making. I went out onto the front balcony of the ranch-style house they had built and moved into the same year I left home for university. The house always felt a bit strange to me; their home not mine. I stood in the dusk, hands on the railing, thinking I ought to join my father in the back garden where he was sitting in a lawn chair, but what would we say? So I waited—enjoying the gathering darkness, the racing clouds on the horizon, the white spirea below and the red tiles underfoot, cool as I expected, once I came inside and unlaced my shoes.

I went out back in bare feet and sat in the folding chair next to him. I told him the train service was being reduced, there would be fewer trains between Toronto and London. It made him sad, as I knew it would. It made me sad too. We sat under the blossoming black locust near a ground cover made fragrant by the approaching rain and could not think of another thing to say to each other.

By this time my father was a professor of education at the university on the other side of town. In Owen Sound he had been a history teacher, well liked, much admired. In Wiarton he was the feared high school principal, desperately trying to find staff when teachers were in short supply, and being above all an administrator and disciplinarian. It took me a long time to appreciate how hard he worked, even though I could see that he was always at his desk in the evening and on weekends, preparing the classes he continued to teach, drawing up timetables, dealing with the school board, marking papers and so on. For years he spent chunks of every summer marking history exams in Toronto, and it was restful to have him out of the picture; a family recess, if you like. Those were the days in Ontario when Grade Thirteen students wrote province-wide examinations and teachers across the province congregated in the steamy big city to get all the marking done. My father was also intent upon getting a master's degree in education and becoming a professor, so he took summer courses at the University of Toronto. He was a driven man, never satisfied with himself, never, in his estimation, the equal of his older brother, who had a master's degree in history—to my father's mind, a real and challenging subject. My father considered his brother Alex's the greater achievement by far, considered his brother's brains far superior to his own, even though this brother, my uncle Al, was content to spend his entire teaching career in the same private Quaker school in a small town in Pennsylvania.

My father was older now. Hearty, healthy, but getting old. And good to us: he wouldn't have dreamed of leaving any of us in the lurch. A responsible man, who believed we should do our best.

And yet the baleful contempt.

The next afternoon I heard what sounded like rain, looked up and saw him taking the wash down off the line. I considered getting up to help, but he was almost done. I continued to read.

When he came in, I looked up, thanked him for getting the clothes, expressed surprise at the rain.

"What did you think that pitter patter was?" he said.

"I didn't notice it."

"Oh. You must be concentrating." Then the sardonic dig: "At least, I'd like to *think* that's the reason."

We were two honest people, in the main, who could not be straightforward with each other.

The progress of love, I thought later, recalling Alice Munro's title as I pondered our cloudy exchange about the rain, in which he and I had managed to make me disingenuous once again: a sneak. The rocky progress of love, as I watched my mother weep in the kitchen. I had said to her, "He never has anything good to say about himself, he never has anything good to say about us." And she, "That's not true, he's so damned proud of all of you, and of me too." She wept as she repeated, "You just don't know, you have no idea. You have no idea."

She gave me examples of how he had burst into tears when each of us had done various things: an award for most Christian camper that my oldest brother received (she called it an award for human excellence, being no fan of Christianity) and my sister's performance of a piece of music. "He had to leave the room, he was in tears." She had no example for me, yet I believed her. Why wouldn't I? I was as filled with self-esteem as my father, the kind of self-esteem that springs leaks at every turn.

That night I lay awake in the spare room, across the hall from their room, fighting with him in my mind. Another of his comments had lodged, and in the darkness it was the only thing in my head. At dinner I had repeated a friend's good joke: that I looked exactly like Wayne Gretzky, except he wears more jewellery.

My mother laughed, but my father didn't even smile. He said, "He certainly has more talent."

My mother looked at him and said gently, "In hockey."

But he stared straight ahead, ignoring her.

In the morning, after my wakeful night and before he appeared for breakfast, Mom asked me how I had slept and I told her, and told her why. Then once we were all together at the breakfast table, she said, "The two of you should have a dialogue instead of fighting in your sleep."

"You were fighting with me?" I asked him, struck by a ray of hope that I counted for something in his thoughts too.

He said, "I dreamt I'd been made principal of the collegiate in Owen Sound."

"And you were fighting with me?"

"No."

"Well, I was with you." And I referred to his crack about no talent, but jokingly. "I want a compliment a day."

"And honesty at the same time?" he said, again without a trace of a smile.

I knew I would have to choose my moment carefully because I would get only one chance. When did you first see Dad lose his temper? Before you were married or after? If my tone was critical rather than curious, if I made my mother defensive, then I had no hope of getting the spontaneous truth. It would take a trusting, easy expansiveness on my part and also on hers. The moment needed to flow from a mood of unguarded intimacy into this further cave, the deep cavern where words never went. And so I hesitated and put off asking the question one more time.

It's not that my mother never allowed dissatisfaction with him to pass her lips. Once, over the telephone, she said to me that his negative view of himself, so deeply entrenched, was "unconstructive." And there was one occasion, one only, when she told me she had considered leaving him. She was harking back to the summer of 1984, when her studio got built onto the side of the house and afterwards the two of them laid the floor of terracotta tiles. I gathered he was particularly abusive over that two-week stretch. I'm talking verbal abuse, not physical, toward my mother. His harsh rebukes and flaring impatience ate into her. He bullied; she brooded. She did not leave him, of course. Her loyalty was oceanic and she had almost no income of her own.

He had a streak of melancholy, my father, the way some people have a streak of meanness. In these wet, dark days leading up to what is bound to be a green Christmas, I entertain myself by imagining the look on his face if he were to go to the window. He would survey the infernal wetness with baggy eyes and pronounce the day revolting, then turn his back on it and grimace at the floor. Nobody, and I mean nobody, took the weather more personally.

Growing up, the weather vane I watched like a hawk was his generous lower lip. It swung into action—trembling, swelling, jutting out—moments before the actual storm hit. Once that lip began to tremble, I went still. We all did.

There was something sexual about it, about this aroused man, not that he ever laid a sexual hand on me. Still, anger was a piece of a sexual puzzle. My father's anger was. My father was.

In old age his regular complaint became that he wished he could be of more use. Rather than be of use, he complained he wasn't of use. In his wing chair, among the African violets, watered at most once a week, my mother told me, or they'll rot, he sat feeling repelled by himself for being so much like his father.

"He couldn't catch a ball if you handed it to him on a silver platter," he said once. "I was disgusted with him, to tell the truth."

Yet to his chagrin he saw himself becoming more and more like him, more silent, more passive, a part of the woodwork, and less and less like his sociable, vivacious mother, who was the one who drove the car in that family, Conran dusting off the hood with his handkerchief before Gracie got behind the wheel.

"You have a lot of your father in you," Mark said to me once. We were on one of our trips to the family cabin at the lake in eastern Ontario. It was late September, and my eyes gravitated to the colours in the hills, mostly yellow with flashes of orange, as thoughts of my parents pressed in and darkened the air around me—even though they were safely in London. We would be alone at the cabin.

"Like what?"

"Your desire to be left alone."

"What else?"

"Your temper."

"What else?"

"You hate talking on the telephone."

"I have his nose."

"Of course. We mustn't forget that."

"What else?"

"His love of language."

The unexpected answer. "What do you mean, love of language?"

"At least once a day he talks about some word he's been thinking about."

"You mean a word he can't remember?"

"A word that interests him."

I had never noticed. I had always thought of us banging our heads against words, but there must have been love there, somewhere. How often had I seen him at his end of the dining room table lower his head into his hands and berate himself for forgetting some word or its meaning. The same dining room table where doing my homework I'd had mental seizures as words eluded me, blackguard words taunted me. In high school I kept a notebook listing definitions, and it killed me that I could never remember the goddamn meaning of "atavistic."

My father, the man of few words who loved words. He had the deepest, scariest, most resonant voice. The sound of his feet used to carry too, the heels of his shoes equipped with metal clickers that struck terror into the hearts of students hearing him approach. His insults were legion, and it gives me particular pleasure to write them down: doughhead, knuckle-head, dimwit, nitwit, stupid head, bonehead, numbskull, dim bulb, meathead, stupid nit, stupid twit, dumb cluck, fathead, nincompoop, lame brain, hambone, hole in the head. Perhaps I've missed a few.

At the lake, inside the dark cabin that was steeped in my parents' lives, I felt permeated by their presence even though they were absent. That a peaceful place should be so full of tension, that their influence should be so potent, that I could not prevent myself from taking on certain of their characteristics and that these same characteristics expanded inside me until I was bloated with impatience, hard with gassy vile severity.

"Even when they're not here!" I cried to Mark.

"But they *are* here."

"You mean hovering about?"

I felt them hovering. I saw their ghostlike forms.

"No. I mean inside your head."

Ah.

"Let them out," he said. "Let them out."

I went to the window and saw my father at the picnic table as he had been earlier in the summer, a man too brightly lit, an old man overexposed, a northerner blinking in the sun-baked heat, an old man in shorts hesitating at a restaurant door, a weak old man who didn't even know what a black birch was. He identified the tree to me in his no-discussion way, only for me to learn later from Stu that what Dad called black birch was, in fact, yellow birch. He wanted respect and adoration, and was puzzled and hurt and full of self-pity that more of each did not come his way. I won't adore you. I won't adore you. And I won't indulge you either.

"Don't you see his fun-loving side?" my mother protested time and time again, trying to get me to soften. I would shake my head at her, hating the way he used to come up behind me as I did the dishes and jab me in the ribs, then laugh in that jeering way when I turned around in wrath.

I cleaned the cabin for an hour, sweeping the large rattan rug and the large, equally old red rug that covered the rest of the cabin floor, beating the brains out of the collection of little mats that lay on the plywood floor next to the bunk beds, misshapen filthy bilious strays—I knocked them silly against the big hemlock outside. Only after twenty-four hours did the stranglehold begin to loosen. Not in the cabin itself, but on the water, and then more generally. By the time we left two days later, I was taking stock of all the things from my child-hood that were living a tranquil second life in the woods, my dresses turned into pillowcases, brass candlesticks burdened with wax, sleeping bags generations old, ancient shoes and boots, and all the old cutlery and mismatched dishes and cups that had graduated to this place of higher shade.

My mother told me once that when my father first brought her home to meet his parents, she took one look at his father and thought, What on earth will our children look like? Conran Hay was small and homely, without an extra scrap of flesh on his bones. He had a long, narrow face with a great beaked nose, large floppy ears, and an ever-present pipe in his mouth. In time she would get into the habit of removing his glasses from his head and polishing them clean. "You could have made a meal from what was on those glasses," she said. Gracie, on the other hand, was robust and pretty, with abundant white hair and a definite sense of style; she never failed to change from her day dress into a better dress for dinner, and kept to a colour scheme of blues and purples.

My grandparents fell in with the Quakers only after coming to Canada. They emigrated from the north of England, outgoing Gracie having been raised in the rigid sect known as the Plymouth Brethren, and introspective Conran having been active in establishing the Young Men's Christian Association in Manchester as a way to improve the lives of the poor. So my father was raised in the pacifist Religious Society of Friends, a community of people who were always dropping by, being fed, staying over. He was pulled along happily in the tailwinds of their sociability, a part of something larger than himself and larger than family, this companionable way of walking humbly with the Lord. In the small Ontario towns where I grew up, there were no Quaker meeting houses, but when I went to university in Toronto I attended from time to time the Friends' meeting for worship on Lowther Avenue. My life was coloured by Quaker influences for a decade or so. Ultimately, I chafed against what I took to be their coercive goodness and turned away.

Only recently, my thoughts about Quakers and my father received a jolt so unexpected it swung my views around. I was rereading *Wuthering Heights*, giving it yet another go, since for all my bluster I've always found it too disturbing and Heathcliff too cruel, too weird to be romantic, and preferred *Jane Eyre*, which gave me someone to love and admire with all my heart, namely Jane. I started with V.S. Pritchett's introduction and soon I was reading about my father, for Pritchett writes about the people in the north of England being of a "blunt, opinionated disposition . . . brutal in their habit of outspoken truthfulness which, on their lips, sounds and *is* combative and merciless." "They are great haters," he says, and reminds us that in Yorkshire "it must be remembered that George Fox, the Quaker mystic who saw visions of towns bathed in blood, had his greatest success." And suddenly it occurred to me that what Quakerism provided for these people of strong temperament was a release from drastic anger into a vision of the light within, simple and overwhelming and direct, uncluttered by the trappings of the steeple houses George Fox loved to despise. Here he is, in 1656, exhorting on behalf of simplicity and Truth: "Be patterns, be examples in all countries, places, islands, nations, wherever you come, that your carriage and life may preach among all sorts of people, and to them; then you will come to walk cheerfully over the world, answering that of God in every one."

My sister never feared our father the way I did. There was the unforgettable morning when she was five or six years old, standing on the far side of the kitchen, and he ordered her to come here to be spanked for something she had done or said, some disobedient act, *here* being where he was standing in the doorway in his winter coat and boots. She responded with a "No!" and stoutly held her ground. Her temerity and Dad's reaction astounded me. His arms went slack at his sides and his head tilted back in helpless laughter.

My fear, on the other hand, rubbed his face in what he had done. Had I not been afraid, he would not have been reminded so constantly of incidents he was ashamed of. But I did remind him, and he was ashamed, and angrier for not being allowed to forget. Every time he teased me, then teased harder to get back at me for not laughing, my reaction reminded him that he had a touchy, humourless daughter, that she was afraid of him, that she had reason to be afraid, that he was ashamed of his temper, yet took a not-so-secret pleasure in it.

I recall him swinging his briefcase (a hard reinforced tan leather case) like a scythe at Stu's head, who managed to duck in time. And on an earlier occasion, dragging the same brother, dear peace-loving Stu, across the kitchen and throwing him this way and that—Stu's screams, my mother's frantic, protesting face—and kicking him up the back stairs.

I recall him knocking a boy in my class across the head with his hand. "Did you see that?" my classmates said all around me. "Did you see that?" Dad had been patrolling the hall and through the small window in the classroom door spotted the boy throwing chalk while the teacher was out of the room, wheeled back, strode in like your worst nightmare and grabbed that boy by the scruff of the neck. "So you like throwing chalk, do you?" And he hammered him on the head with his hand, shoved him across the room, shook him into the hall. The hush afterwards. And then the shocked voices all around me.

"Why are you so *belligerent*?" my mother would ask me.

The lesson she taught, I believed at the time, was peace at any cost. When my father lost his temper, he didn't really mean it. When he rode me, he was only having fun. And when I defended myself, I was belligerent.

So we argued, my mother and I, about memories, and the moment never seemed right to ask my question. She was too busy defending him. "He was just ribbing you, why can't you laugh?" she said for years. *Just ribbing you.* As if he had some right to. Women created as we were.

My anger when I was growing up was nasty, uncooperative, curdled, whereas his, though explosive, was not a state of mind. He glutted himself on bad temper and felt better, while his children were left like a flattened field of hay.

Something changed when I had children myself. Then I met my own awful appetite for punishment and was appalled at myself, appalled at him in me.

During one of my visits to London, I yanked two-year-old Sochi's hand away, dirty with food, when she put it on my shoulder, and she burst into tears. The same thing happened when she grabbed my braid.

"I could have thrown her against the wall," I said to my father after she was finally napping in the spare room and we were at the table together. I shook my head, tense, exasperated, increasingly so all day. But also, in that moment, playing up to him, implying we were cut from the same cloth and understood each other.

"Don't worry about it," he said to me, and on his face was the unguarded, caring, thoughtful look he had when he was at his best. "Unless you throw her against the wall," he added ruefully, "and then you'll have to worry."

My mother said, "We're familiar with spasms of anger too."

Without any of us saying it, we were all back in the same place, the dining room in Owen Sound.

I shook my head again and stared down at my plate.

"You don't remember?" my father said, as if it were possible.

"Oh, I do. I do."

And that was our conversation. At the time, it was enough. The acknowledgement that he worried when he threw us. The hope that I had forgotten. My quick assurance that I had not. And my mother's acknowledgement—finally—that it wasn't simply an accident. It seemed enough.

Years passed and I didn't ask my question. In truth, it was more than one question, as I must have known. The first led to the next, which led in turn to the ultimate accusation. When did you first see him lose his temper? Were you afraid too? Is that why you didn't defend me?

The thought that my mother was also afraid never entered my head until I was in my forties. I was standing over the stove, clattering a lid onto a saucepan, a sound that called my mother immediately to mind, for in my nervousness that supper would be late, I felt her endless tension as she worked to meet my father's expectations.

She oiled his moody wheels. Never once did she protest when he struck me. Never once did she come to my defence when I was growing up.

Then out of that dark mess, I came to love her with a passion.

It happened one summer when my father was away. It

must have been when he and his brother, Alex, took their long trip together on the Trans-Siberian Railway. I had been gone since September, attending university, and returned in May to spend the summer working in a market garden. For all of June and July, I saw my mother on her own day after day. In that atmosphere of summer freedom doubled by my father's absence, we talked about art and books and artistic aspirations, and I fell for this kindred spirit, my endlessly creative mother.

My question went unasked, as I say. We saw my parents on holidays, usually with other members of the family, and I could never summon up the necessary even-handed tone. They got older and older, until they were very old.

In early October 2008, a month before disaster struck, I paid them a visit by myself. We sat in their back garden on folding chairs that we kept shifting into the receding sunshine. A sharp and sizable hump between my mother's shoulder blades told the story of the compression fractures that had turned their summer into a long misery, although by now she was down to two pain pills a day from four.

In the evening my father uncharacteristically fell into a long reminiscence. We moved from the dining room into the kitchen, the dishes got done, and he stood on the other side of the counter and talked about summers past, more forthcoming and relaxed with me than perhaps he had ever been before. He talked about the excellent teachers he had had in high school, one of whom went on to become ambassador to Russia, others, he said, who should have been university professors, but it was the Depression and therefore the headmaster at his private Quaker school near Toronto was able to hire them and hold on to them for a time. His admiration for these teachers was complete. Of Bob Rourke, his math and science teacher, he said, "You couldn't have got anyone better." He reminisced about the job he had for five summers as a boat boy on Lake Joseph in the Muskokas working for Andy "Pop" Davis, who owned Davis Leather in Newmarket; a rich man. His wife, Audrey, was an invalid with a heart condition, so Pop had an elevator installed for her in their Newmarket home, and on Lake Joe she and her nurse occupied their own cottage. Dad said that he called Andy Davis "Pop" and he called Audrey "Mom," and they all ate at the same table. Pop also had a chauffeur. At the end of the season, when the summer house was officially closed up, Pop would bring his chauffeur, his gardener and his boat boy up for a weekend of euchre. The cottage next to Pop's, much smaller, was owned by the Kemps, whose daughter, Helen, went on to marry Northrop Frye. So my athletic father was witness to the famous-scholar-and-critic-to-be trying to paddle a canoe. He could not have been less impressed.

His account of living with wealth drew from my mother thoughts of her own family's hard times after her father died and left behind nothing but uncollected debts. "I didn't give my mother any concessions," she said. "I was too occupied with my own warp in the world. I knew there were two categories, the rich and the poor. No, there was a third category. People who had been well off and weren't anymore. That was us."

When it came time to turn in for the night, I said that I would see them in the morning, and my father said, "It's a sad day for us. To see you go. But a good day for Mark."

I am very glad I wrote that down in my notebook. I would not have remembered it otherwise, so uniform is the dark cloud I carry around with me. I see him standing in the kitchen doorway, grateful for my company, having taken uncommon pleasure in recalling those years in his past when he knew and appreciated a wealthy man but never thought of seeking wealth himself; rather, he would be a teacher and hope to earn the kind of admiration he felt for the admirable teachers in his own life.

I had listened with surprise and pleasure, asking questions to draw him out, but not truly comfortable with him, not even then. I could see how lonely he was, how starved for company. I knew that he and my mother had entered a very vulnerable time.

Around five o'clock the next morning, a loud crash woke me out of a sound sleep. I heard his voice. Then Mom's answer, "Here."

She had fallen in the hallway as she turned to go into the kitchen (to check the time on the clock above the kitchen window) and cracked the back of her head against the carved wooden chest that stood at the head of the stairs. She sat on the floor, stunned but lucid, as an enormous goose egg materialized on the back of her head. I got her a glass of water and sat with her, while Dad returned to their bedroom and got dressed. In those years of her decline, he had a way of staying by her side and removing himself from the picture, supportive and critical, steady and distant. She chose to believe in one side of him more than the other. And I suppose so did I.

After a few more minutes, she worked her feet over to the staircase and used the railing to haul herself upright. I helped her stand and felt the curving C of her bending carcass, so thin, small, humped from osteoporosis. Later, after breakfast, we went for a walk around the block, and she took three long pauses to rest. She leaned first against a tree, then a low pillar, then a car. I went back to get her a bottle of water during the third pause. "'The relief of Maeve,'" she said gratefully when I unscrewed the cap and handed her the water. A phrase from a poem memorized as a girl, but neither the title nor its author could she call up.

That same morning, we sat on the edge of her bed and she put drops in my dry, itchy eyes, as she had been putting anti-glaucoma drops in my father's eyes for a dozen years or more. Her practised hands were so precise.

We were by ourselves. My father was far away in the living room. "Mom?" I said. "When was the first time you saw Dad lose his temper?"

The words were finally out.

Her expression grew fractionally more thoughtful. She gazed out the bedroom window that overlooked the garden. "Well, we were well and truly married."

My heart quickened. But no, she proceeded to describe something I already knew, the time in Owen Sound when he packed the car to go to West Hill, one of their trips to see Conran and Gracie, and had been impatient with her for being slow to get ready. "Everyone was in the car," she said. "Very quiet. We all were *quiet*." He started to back the car out of the garage, only to be stopped by a loud thud; he had packed the roof rack higher than the garage door. She smiled at the memory, and with that amused light touch of hers said confusingly that he got out and lowered the garage door and the night's accumulated rainwater came down on his head.

I had waited too long. She was mixing up two frequently told and safe stories, the sort of life-with-father stories that drove me nuts because they always ended with "and to his everlasting credit, he laughed." She dwindled to a stop.

Neither the roof rack nor the rainwater was about his first

explosion of anger, which had mended itself like patched trousers into other things, into the hand-stitched fabric of my mother's peace-loving mind.

"I waited too long," I said a couple of months later. "There was a question I wanted the answer to, but I waited too long to ask it."

My son's eyes lit up with interest. "What question?"

Mark had been telling us about my father's rancor and rudeness with my sister, who had said something innocuous and he had rounded on her, "And what do you know about it, you stupid twit." Even though the physiotherapist was right there, working with my mother, a few feet away. Later, my sister called Dad into the kitchen and told him that if he had something to say to her, he should say it now. He hung his head and walked away. Mark's account had left me struck once again by how well my sister dealt with my father.

"I wanted to know if Mom knew that he had a violent temper before she married him. I asked her one day. I sat down beside her on the edge of the bed and asked her when she first saw him get angry, and she started in on these over-worn stories, all of them harmless, and she got confused as she told them."

Ben said, "It's hard to remember first times of things."

"Ask the question in another way," Mark suggested. "Did you know he had a violent temper when you married him?"

"I couldn't say violent. She would see that as an attack on him."

"A temper. Did you know he had a temper before you got married?"

I shook my head. My mother's mind was at sea. It was too late. We would never have a full and lucid conversation about my father's anger, and how it had shadowed and shaped us both.

Yet now, half a dozen years after those events, I see there was a lot in her drifting answer. "We were well and truly married," she had said. And then came her eloquent description of our cowed silence. "We all were *quiet*."

Yes, that is exactly how it was, time and time again. We all were *quiet*. The bear was loose.

Here's a truth I had almost forgotten. We were proud of his temper. So long as it wasn't directed at us, we admired it as you might admire an active volcano. Even now when I read about the north-of-Englanders who responded so keenly to George Fox, I pity those of a milder disposition. My father's intemperate aggressiveness, like our dog Jet's, we considered manly and impressive. He liked to let rip.

He never knew, and neither did my mother, that when I was a student in his school and my classmates one day were complaining bitterly to the teacher about some decision he had taken, I raised my hand to defend him and to my horror out of my mouth spilled the word "Daddy." I had meant to say "my father." Beet-red, hideously embarrassed, I nevertheless stood up for him. In my anguished way I was proud of him, but what is pride in such circumstances?

There was a moment, a scene, in the last summer of his life. On a hot afternoon we drove my parents from the retirement home to a lake in the Gatineau Hills, where we sat on the verandah of an old lodge and looked across the water to the far shore of tall, unbroken trees. A storm blew up. We watched it gather force from inside the screened porch, my mother intent and eager, her face glowing, while my father pressed his back against the sofa, not wanting to get wet. After the storm died down, a friend—there were friends there too—leaned across to him and said, "You must be very proud of your daughter." He didn't hear, or pretended not to. Knowing how unwelcome this kind of facile praise was to my father, I waved my hands to silence my friend. But he repeated himself, louder, leaning closer to my father.

Looking neither left nor right, my father snapped back, "Is she proud of me? If she's proud of me, then I'm proud of her."

What a pair we were, withholding approval from each other.

I enjoyed his answer, mostly. He wasn't about to indulge in any sappy, simpleminded guff. Instead, he gave me something to think about. He gave me himself to think about. But it meant we were left waiting for a word from each other that never came.

WHEN ICEBERGS MELT

IN THEIR LAST YEARS in London I used to wash my mother's hair for her whenever I went to visit. It hurt her to raise her arms above her head, the result of a shoulder injury a few years earlier when she had lost her balance on a train. She would lead the way into the bathroom and set up an electric heater on the floor and get it blasting before shedding her vest, her sweater, her shirt, everything but a thin-strapped undergarment of dubious origin. Her loose skin hung off her bones like silken parchment. She filled the sink with warm water, then bent over it while I stood behind her and ran cupfuls of water over her head. I shampooed and rubbed, then worked her scalp with my fingertips, the good scrubbing she wanted, feeling in the process her multiple wens like tiny hard nipples on her scalp, about six or eight of them. Wens—more formally they are known as sebaceous cysts—are a family trait on my mother's side. My own are rounder than hers but no less alarming under my fingertips. If you have wens you'll never get brain cancer, or so went the Ottawa Valley folk wisdom my mother passed on to me, just as she comforted me about the size of my nose by briskly saying, "You'll age well." I was thirteen at the time and had been staring gloomily into the mirror.

I rinsed, conditioned, rinsed again and wrapped her head in a towel. She emptied the sink. We wiped up all the water. I lifted the heater onto the counter and trained it on her hair as she sat on the toilet lid, combing and brushing her soft crown of silvery-white.

It was on such a visit to them, two years before she landed in hospital, that I became aware of how little of my parents was left. It was late July. Without their winter layers of fleece and flannel and wool, they were bone-thin, minor wisps of themselves. My mother's bare arms were as pitiable as a ballerina's. My father's famously fine legs came out of his shorts like sticks. (In their joint prime, my mother used to openly admire his strong thighs and shapely calves, her painter's eye as gratified as her wifely pride. Certainly when my father wore the briefest of swimming briefs, in 1950s style, we all got an eyeful.) Despite the extreme heat, my mother could not get warm. She went around closing all the windows against the summer breezes. Here was personal climate change every bit as radical as what was happening to our planet. I watched with sorrow and alarm as she moved around the house, a crooked, cane-needy old woman, one shoulder much higher than the other. She was eighty-six. They both were.

On her easel was a long-unfinished painting of lichens growing on white quartz. She was using a technique called impasto to convey the different angles and dimensions of the quartz, working in fits and starts from a photograph she had taken years before at the northern end of Ellesmere Island. Puzzled at first by the lines of dirt in the clefts of the stone, she had realized after examining them with a magnifying glass that they were not dirt at all, but black lichens in the very earliest stages of growth. "And that had tremendous meaning for me."

I slept in my father's study downstairs to get off the beaten path to the bathroom and away from his alarm clock, which split the air at 7 a.m. as it had every day of his working life.

His study had a wall of books, and I pulled two of them off the shelf and took them to bed with me. *Finding the Trail of Life* by the Quaker Rufus Jones: "poetry and art and religion, which are as old as smiling and weeping"; and *A Fiddler's World* by Harry Adaskin: "Kafka said there is perhaps only one cardinal sin—impatience. Certainly the great doers and shakers of the world, who have killed millions of people, and are doing it right now, are guilty of *that* sin. But why are they so impatient? They're impatient because they are *unaware* that spiritual growth, which is the only direction we can hope for, cannot come quickly."

I fell asleep on the thought that impatience is also as old as smiling and weeping.

I returned during another heat wave in September, the time of hurricanes in more operatic parts of the world. On the first day of my visit, rain and wind shook off some of the heat, but then it turned steamy again, day and night, until a shift in the wind brought sheets of cold stiff rain. My parents turned on the furnace, and I became aware of a mighty change in my own life: that of being uncomfortably warm in my parents' house. Had I only known that all the freezing hours of my childhood would lead to this, *removing* my sweater in the presence of my formidable parents, had I only known the punchline that lay in store, imagine how good-tempered I might have been when I was young.

I went back again in December and we talked about how to identify the years in the first decade of a new century, still a topic in letters to the editor even if it was already 2006. One letter-writer offered Jane Austen's solution: in *Persuasion*, Captain Wentworth, who liked to talk, said, "That was in the year six; That happened before I went to sea in the year six." Another remembered his grandparents saying "oh-six" and writing it as '06. I don't recall my parents having a preference. I rather think we shared the view that nothing so elegant as "'06" or "the year six" would become current usage in our chaotic day.

Several of my mother's northern paintings were on the walls around us. Under our hands were placemats stitched by her from rescued material she had come by somehow or other, the sort of flowered fabric popular in the shifts women wore in the 1960s. They made splashes of tropical colour on the dark mahogany table that, like their double bed, had come to Canada with Gracie and Conran's furnishings when they emigrated from Manchester in 1912.

This talk of the past prompted my father to say the reason he knew all the makes of cars when he was a boy was because of collecting the automobile cards in cans of tobacco. His father smoked a brand called Macdonald's. He then surprised me by referring to his mother's darkroom.

"Darkroom?" Wondering how that could be. "You mean Gracie developed her own photographs?"

She did. She was the first in her circle to have a camera. Her brother Harold would have provided the equipment, and Uncle Hugh the know-how. "And my father," he said, "would have been useless."

"He's talking about George," I said to my mother, and we shared a knowing smile about his entrenched disregard for the quiet, impractical father he had nicknamed George.

This was the moment, as I remember it, when I felt my father's disappointment in his father as lifelong pain rather than mere intolerance. It entered my bones, his profound alienation from one parent, which bolstered his deep love for the other. The Uncle Hugh he admired was a family friend, a courtesy uncle, and, in my father's view, much more suited to Gracie than his father ever was; he even suspected a hidden love between them, or at least a cherishing of his mother on the part of Hugh Marshall. I had entertained for many years a similar notion, pondering what my mother's life would have been like had she married someone less difficult to live with. Had she married Uncle Al, my father's good-humoured brother, say, instead of my father.

During that visit I slept again in his study on the ground floor, protected by the books that couldn't help but make me aware of what was easy to forget: that he was more of a searcher and a yearner than his tyrannical disposition made him appear. He knew cars and he knew sports, yet he was the one with the spiritual books on his shelves. *Christian Faith and Practice in the Experience of the Society of Friends*, Dag Hammarskjold's *Markings*, Schweitzer's *Reverence for Life*. Plus many books on Canadian and British history, as well as books of philosophy and a dozen or more old school readers he had collected over the years. Lying awake on the single bed built into the wall, I thought of him heading upstairs for meals and my mother coming in from her studio, in from outside really, since her windowed studio jutted out into the garden, while his desk was subterranean, the one window made smaller by the overbearing yews that pressed against the glass. On his desk lay notes he had made while reading, his penmanship like a series of rolling waves, whereas my mother's handwriting was minuscule, allowing her to get more words on a page than Seurat got dots on a canvas.

They were like an iceberg, it occurred to me, my father the seven-eighths that was under the water and my mother the luminous portion riding the waves. But no, they were two icebergs: solitary phenomena, impressive, independent, known only to themselves. I felt their hidden seven-eighths inside me as a dark bulkiness whose outlines I was always trying to map. They kept to their separate parts of the bay, except when they came together in the kitchen and then at the dining room table, which had icy undertones of its own, having been shipped across the Atlantic in the same fateful April that the *Titanic* met its doom.

With each successive visit more of them had melted away. Now I often knew more details about my mother's past than she did. Her first memory, of being carried in her father's arms to the top of Blimkies Mountain in the Ottawa Valley and set down among the blueberries he picked into her hands, extended into a later memory, nine years after his death, of being sixteen and escaping her family for a weekend alone at their cabin on Hurds Lake. She set about picking enough blueberries to make a pie (the picking took hours, she had told me) with the intention of eating the whole pie herself, only for her three older brothers and her mother to turn up on the doorstep as her hard-won creation sat cooling on the table. They proceeded to gobble it down in front of her eyes.

"Why didn't you hide it?" I had wanted to know, for she had told me the story with considerable asperity—her plans ruined by her ravaging family, her life flayed open by their intrusiveness. As soon as I asked my question, she made light of her resentment. She hadn't really meant to eat the entire pie herself, her family wasn't so bad, the incident hadn't gnawed away at the back of her mind for nigh on sixty years.

I would have hidden it had I thought I could get away with it. But there would have been the telltale aroma, some evidence of my subterfuge, there always was, on which I would have been skewered, and then I would have spun around on my skewer like a chunk of slipshod meat.

I considered that story typical of my mother's caving in: anything to keep the peace and appear to be good. Yes, a certain passion, a certain passionate resentment, but never to be acted upon. Always to be softened by forgiving laughter.

I didn't want her to make light of her anger. I wanted her to do something ferocious.

In my childhood we all got our fair share. Cherries she counted out scrupulously and distributed as we sat on the verandah. Cake she sliced "even steven." Spoonfuls of whipped cream made matching plops on the six servings of jello. And so on. I remember her anger once when she thought a handful of sesame seeds, left in the wake of a dozen bagels, had been tossed out, then her pleasure when she discovered they had been eaten. She used to make applesauce in quantity from the fruit of our old apple trees. It fermented slowly over the winter in big glass jars in the cold cellar, until by spring the sauce had a kick like a burro. She would skim off the thick layer of whitish-blue mould and ladle the sauce into our bowls for breakfast, taking our complaints in fairly good humour until the morning when Al, then about twenty and home for Easter perhaps, protested too long. She got up from her chair, chuckling, went around to his side of the table, lifted the bowl of applesauce and pressed it right into his face. Chuckling still, she removed the bowl. Globs of sauce slid down his cheeks, now scarlet from his own shocked laughter.

I have to admit that was pretty ferocious.

The most interesting thing about this story is that no one else remembered it when I recalled the details one Christmas morning many years later. My mother didn't remember. The applesauce-smeared brother didn't remember. My other brother said, "The trouble with that story is that Mom would never waste applesauce." But it wasn't wasted. She scraped it off his face back into the bowl for him to eat, and he ate.

Here is my favourite story about my mother's food. I was in my thirties and we were outside, sitting in folding chairs in their sunny garden with bowls of soup in our laps. I swallowed several spoonfuls, then said, "There are worms in the soup."

"Really? I thought I got them all out."

A packaged soup mix, partially used a dozen years before by my sister in her shared apartment at university, then packed into a box along with other odds and ends when she moved back home. Stored in the kitchen cupboard, it had become a mating ground for little white worms, each a quarter of an inch long.

The next day my mother served the same soup. "I'm not going to eat it," I said.

"Oh?" Mildly disappointed that I wasn't willing to play along. And to my father, "You can either eat the soup with worms or fish the worms out into the sink."

"How about throwing the soup out?" he said.

"You can't throw out perfectly good food."

And so my father meekly stood over the sink and fished out the worms.

Later, I related the incident to a friend, expecting her to laugh, and her response rocked me. "That's insane," she said, taking a step back. "She is mentally ill."

I realized then that this was not a story I could tell. No one would understand. They would miss the point of my mother's character. They would over-salt her somehow and not get the true flavour. Only someone who knew her and loved her would see the humour in the implacability of her nature.

I'm telling the story now, though. Serving your family worms. My mother forced her will on us in horrible ways.

In their last two years in London, every meal, it seemed, was punctuated by her cry of distress. Not, "What is happening to poor me?" Rather, "What is going to become of our poor planet?"

Our eyes would turn to her anguished face. What could we say that we had not said before? We tried to bring a sense of proportion to her torment, or change the subject altogether. But she kept returning to the ruination of the environment, she could not help herself. My father stared down at his place-mat, moved his knife and fork around, pursed his lips. It was easy to think her lament was nothing but her love of nature, rather than what it turned out to be, at least in part: the repetitive, incessant, exhausting workings of old-fashioned senility. My father understood this before the rest of us.

I precipitated one of their exchanges during a visit to them in June of 2008. My mother's love of *Moby-Dick* had shamed me into finally reading the book, and at the dining room table I said that Melville needed an editor. He created fabulous characters, I said, then dropped them, so the novel sank under the weight of his endless whale discursions.

My mother said, "You're missing the point."

My father said, "What is the point?"

"That animals are as important as humans."

"This is what I was afraid of," he said.

"Life on this planet," my mother said.

Here we go again, his exasperated face said. "So what?" he replied. "What will be will be. It's beyond us. It's out of our hands."

I intervened. "But you spent your life trying to make a better world," I said to him.

"Yes. But that's over."

"So what would you have her think about instead?"

"Use your brain to be here *now*. Not worry about the future. There's nothing you or I"—he looked at my mother—"can do about it."

Our conversation that day shifted to other subjects. She tried to remember something, but it wouldn't come. She closed her eyes in silent fury at her memory. Eyes still closed, "Damn. *Nation.* Piss. *Willy.*"

Heading home with Mark after one of our visits, near Toronto we drove past two people changing a flat tire on the side of the highway, something we had not seen in years. Flat tires had gone the way of dogs running after cars, windshields thick with mashed bugs, children throwing up out of car windows. What my father used to call hopscotch no longer happened—when a car pulled over onto the shoulder either for a child to throw up, or a dog to pee, or a child to pee, and all the cars you had passed would pass you. And then you would set about passing them all over again.

On that long drive did I know that my parents would cover the same distance very soon? That we would move them into a retirement home nearby, where they would be two eroding icebergs sitting in my bay. And almost every day I would row out to see them, and then leave them again for the night. And slowly, over time, they would melt entirely away.

HER MIND

AFTER WE MOVED my parents to Ottawa, what had been my quiet home for seventeen years gained a new set of landmarks: every little dip and rise of the sidewalks and pathways they navigated; the big boulder under the children's climbing tree at the corner church where I found them perched side by side one day; the front gardens they admired; the trees whose names they tried to recall; the familiar flowers my mother claimed she was beholding for the first time. "I've never seen them before," she would say, looking down at marigolds.

She took the lead on their excursions, pushing her walker, hunched over, a crooked leaf. My father brought up the tippy rear. Out of pride he refused a cane for a long, long time.

The six-minute trek on foot from my house to their retirement home turned into a hallway runner under my feet. How strange it was to be walking toward my past, which was also my future: to see what the future held for me, yet to be once again the obedient child. I arrived at their rooms and here were the two vivid giants in my life—still massive no matter how shrunken they had become, while for them I suppose I had grown huge.

Doing errands on foot that first summer, I turned onto Bank Street one day and who should I see coming over the Bank Street Bridge but my father, tilting against the wind, all alone. He was wearing shorts, socks, sandals and a none-too-clean shirt, those once-fine legs of his a spindly set of aged and unreliable toothpicks. So frail that the August wind could have picked him up and blown him the length of the canal, past Parliament Hill and out to the mighty Ottawa River. The expression on his face was hunted, disgruntled. He was escaping my mother's addled mind.

We conferred at the foot of the bridge. "Your mother's jaw is sore," he told me, "she can't eat, and she's talking in a way that makes no sense about having gone to the dentist and the pain from the work on one side of her face having travelled to the other." Infections were scouting out every part of her: knee, bladder, chest and now the jaw. My father was her pillar and her anchor, by her side twenty-four hours a day, and it was driving him around the bend.

He had lost his home, his garden, his study, his car. He hated Ottawa. It was my turf and my mother's turf, not his. He felt the same distaste for some of his fellow inmates, as he took acid pleasure in calling them. Margaret, for instance, the oversized complainer with a stuffed animal in her arms, whose stentorian English accent repelled him. "They should all be *dead*," he said of the old people around him.

Of equal intensity was my mother's abiding fondness for the Ottawa Valley. We would step outside, the two of us, leaving behind the stale retirement-home air that, in a turn of phrase worthy of Samuel Beckett, she called "clogsome in the columns." She would pause to drink in "the beautiful air all four ways around," transported to her hometown of Renfrew sixty miles upriver, where no matter the season the weather was reliable and fresh.

Once, on one of her birthdays, I had asked her what the weather was like the day she was born. She was in her early eighties then, still in London. We were on the telephone and I was looking out my window at the paleness of a November freezing rain, the grey-silk look the trees have when they're coated with ice, the greyer sky behind, and the very wet and crunchy ground onto which the tallest plants in our garden, the pampas grass and the heliotrope and hollyhocks, had toppled. The freezing rain kept up its too-loud rhythms, a crinkly, rustling, plastic-bag sound unlike rain and even less like snow. She said, "I have no idea what hour I was born or what the weather was like. But I know what November twenty-sixth was like, any November twenty-sixth in my childhood. It would have been real winter. Beautiful crisp air and sunny blue skies. We made foot slides on the way to school. You would walk a little ways and then you'd run and slide. You know that. You'd have done the same."

During their first winter and spring in Ottawa, we ploughed from one crisis to another, and I remember how graceful and stoical they were at first, how thankful to their children for piloting them into a safe harbour. And then how cabin fever set in, knotty, rough, claustrophobic, surreal.

Early in February the short, bearded, very capable Scottish doctor who visited the retirement residence twice a week telephoned me to say "some subtle things" indicated that my mother had had a small stroke the day before. "Weakness on the left side of her face," he said, "and her tongue was not quite normal." The most important thing, he emphasized, was getting the medication levels right; he was going to increase her blood thinner.

That same week I went over to pick up my father and take him to the bank and I found her sitting on the edge of the bed, as if sleepy from a nap, straining to speak. "I wonder whether the window. I wonder. The window. Whether. I wonder." A series of words beginning with "w," eerily like the spelling tests she used to give me while braiding my hair beside the kitchen window in Wiarton. ("Where," blowing out her cheeks, "were you when you were wearing your blue dress?" As she brushed my hair with vigorous strokes, then fashioned the French braids and ponytail, her fingers nimble and rapid.)

She was as sleepily confused as the dormouse at the tea party. The doctor came to examine her in the early afternoon, by which time she had pretty well recovered. The next night she was writing a letter to a friend in London. I glanced at the two or three wandering lines and saw that she was talking about winter and repeated "whether" twice, meaning weather. The following day she was in bare feet, bare arms, at her worktable and once again trying to compose letters, struggling to remember names.

Her worktable was the grey Arborite one with the scorch mark at one end that had doubled as kitchen table and ironing board when I was growing up. Now it occupied one corner of their narrow living room. On its surface were scissors, pastels, tubes of paint, pencils, erasers, tracing paper, scrap paper, her sewing kit; but pride of place went to the enlargement of the photograph we had located at the eleventh hour before leaving London. It was the one thing she returned to with something like her old single-minded determination—the planned portrait of Al. So far she had managed to outline on tracing paper the image of her small son fishing, and now that effort lay among rocky attempts to address envelopes. In a letter to Nomie and Wes in London, which she had addressed to Nomie and Fred, she talked about a mother bird circling her head and her fierce efforts to ward it off. An incident I recognized as having happened in the Arctic many years ago, but she wrote in the present tense. It made a kind of entangled sense, but amounted to a very strange communication.

She could not find her address book and blamed Dad for losing it in his desk in the other room. I opened the drawer of the worktable and there it was. "There it is," she said, "there it is. Oh, aren't you wicked. Aren't you wicked." My father she called "the dog." "Do you know what he did, the dog?" she would say, adroitly circumnavigating his exasperation and her forgetfulness with humour and spunk.

In the residence dining room the next day, she said she couldn't remember who she had written to. She remembered putting four envelopes in the mailbox (Dad, in one of his dry asides, said the postman was going to have his work cut out for him deciphering the addresses), but not which friends she had written to.

He said, "Mary Martin was one. Mary has been well written to, or well addressed, at any rate."

He was quite right about that. I had found two envelopes addressed to Mary, their friend going back to Owen Sound days, in one of which was a folded card sent to my mother from another friend in London, and in the other a genuine letter, which I mailed. Later, I found yet another envelope addressed to Mary.

"It's ridiculous," my mother said to me. "It's just ridiculous."

"What is?"

"This ninety-year-old brain of mine."

Around the same time, the middle of February, I arrived in the late afternoon to find her trying to reheat her coffee from lunch. She was outfoxed by the new microwave, and no amount of instruction, verbal or written, was sufficient; my father could not operate it either. In their living room she sat down across from me and demanded, "So what have you been farting around with all day?"

"Well," I said, "I was *here* until two o'clock. Then I helped you lie down for a nap and went home and had some lunch. Then a little walk. And here I am again." Almost as frustrated at not being able to get to my writing as she was at being unable to reconstitute her brains.

There on her worktable was young Al in the timeless and simple pursuit of fishing. He stood with his fishing pole on a boulder at the edge of the sun-drenched river, sturdy bare legs and bare feet, a cloud of flies around him, utterly absorbed: a three-year-old boy in a purposeful trance. The photograph had caught what so disarmed my mother—the essence of her second-born son.

Her earlier pencilled outline had gone into the waste-basket. (I fished it out and kept it, and am looking at its delicate tracery now. It still has something of her old touch, but the next step must have eluded her.) Now she was work-ing directly on the photograph itself, spackling it with white paint. I recognized what she was up to. On my living room wall there is a piece in which she achieved a powdery white effect—a skiff of snow, as she described it—across the surface of kayak and Arctic sea. But in the retirement home she had so little to work with, so few of her tools, so little space, such a scrambled mind that all she was doing was obliterating the photograph under a layer of white. Not the idea of the por-trait, however. That she would keep returning to.

"Have you been writing more letters?" I asked her.

"Words avoid me," she sighed, stating the hard truth and turning away from her half-baked efforts on the table.

Dusk was coming on. Through the window skaters were visible on the canal, and we heard the passage of crows, hundreds if not thousands of them, making their daily flight from their feeding grounds back to wherever they roosted for the night; a sight and sound that fascinated my mother.

Dad asked me if I could stay for supper. "No," I said, itching to make up for lost time. "I have things to do at home."

My father looked hurt. "We'd like you to stay," he said.

"Well, if you put it like that."

So we had supper together in the big dining room downstairs, and later, in their rooms, I witnessed the incident of the card table. In an effort to give my mother space to spread out, my father had set up their temperamental old card table next to her worktable. Now the two surfaces choked that end of the living room. Dad was intent upon her working; he wanted to sit at his desk and write a letter in peace, or read the newspaper in his green wing chair beside the window without being interrupted. This was a turn of events rich in irony, since toward the end of their time in London he had gone to great lengths to keep her out of the studio, ostensibly so she wouldn't overtire, but perhaps to reclaim her for himself. Having set up the card table, he had said to me, "But she doesn't have what she needs." So I had gone to an art supply store and brought back a small stretched canvas. My mother seemed moderately pleased; yes, it was the right size. Was this after my wrangle with Dad, yet again, about the power of attorney? I think it was. With my saying that unless the document was changed to read "jointly and severally," rather than just "jointly," Stu would have to come from Montreal every time we needed to act, which was untenable. "We'll have to see a lawyer," I had said, "to authorize the change."

"That's not going to happen," Dad said.

"Why not?"

"There's no way your mother and I are going to London to see the lawyer."

"We would go to my lawyer in Ottawa."

"No way! My lawyer's in London. I'm not changing lawyers! He's always been my lawyer. Why should I change lawyers?"

But to get back to the card table. On this particular evening, Dad installed himself at his desk and Mom and I went into the living room. She told me she wanted the card table to come down. The pressure of it weighed on her, yet she couldn't bring herself to say so to Dad. I went to tell him, since undoing his work without his permission was unthinkable. He came back with me to where she was standing, arms hanging at her sides. "You're not *doing* any work," he fumed. "You haven't done anything."

"Dad, if she can't do it, she can't do it."

"That's right," he snapped.

Mom, bowed by all this, said simply, "I think the card table should come down."

So Dad, irate, proceeded to fold in its legs, except for the last leg, which wouldn't fold (and hadn't for years). He got hammer and screwdriver from the bottom drawer of their massive chest of drawers, another piece of furniture that had come over from England with his parents. He got down on his knees, but still made no headway. The table sat on its side, its defective and lethal fourth leg sticking halfway across the room, while he was back at his desk, steaming. I tackled it. By using the screwdriver I managed to bring the metal, where it had bent and jammed, out over the hinge.

The following days brought more power-of-attorney madness. In the end we got Dad's lawyer in London involved.

He updated the papers and mailed them to me. I then took them over to the retirement home, where Dad demanded, "What's the difference between this and my will? What was wrong with what I had? Where did all this start?" I led him through it again and again until I was blue in the face.

"Why isn't Al in this?" he demanded.

"Because that's the way you drew it up twelve years ago. You'll have to remember back to why you made Stu and Al executors of your will, and Stu and me power of attorney for financial and personal care."

"I wanted you for personal care, not Stu."

And I had the piercing realization that he must have thought personal care meant bathing and toileting Mom and had nothing to do with decision making of any kind.

There were at least three things at play in this long snafu, which lasted through February and March of that first winter and was only one of many: an old man's confusion, his justifiable wish to be clear about what he was signing, and his lack of faith in me. He refused to sign until the boys saw the papers in person.

The next day I was so tired when I made my trek to their rooms that I was nearly tearful. What was he going to put me through this time? But he was like a lamb, as mild and docile as when he was trying to work himself back into my mother's good graces. Whatever my brothers had said to him on the telephone the previous night had soothed the savage breast. He was ready to sign.

Exaggeration revisited, I think now. But it upset me so. And the old terror dies hard. His rudenesses and explosions were like weather squalls coming through; in an hour they were gone.

He would not apologize, but he felt sorry and would be extra-genial for a bit. But I did not recover so easily.

In early March, my mother fell asleep as she was drinking her coffee at breakfast and spilled it all over herself. My father could not wake her up. Nurses put her in a wheelchair and took her up to my parents' suite on the third floor, where they settled her into her bed. The doctor feared a bleed in the brain and ordered up an ambulance.

Al flew in from Halifax to keep Dad company while Mark and I drove to the Ottawa General Hospital to be with my mother. In the emergency ward, after the battery of doctors with their endless and repetitive questions left us, my mother said to me, "I was aware of being asleep. You'll have to sort this one out. I kept waking up and the thing that woke me up in this period of time we're speaking about was your dad's fading out. I'm seeing several," she said, and didn't go on. Then, "Daylight is dawning," she said, and she began to sing snatches of an old hymn from her childhood. She stopped her singing and repeated, "Daylight is dawning. Then that would snap shut. The daylight was turning and then there'd be a time when it wasn't turning and there'd be the dark part, then Dad's head would be rising with a big smile. It was your dad's smiling face that brought the daylight on with no regard to the actual time that had taken place. And then I'd fall asleep again and this happened five or six times. A distinct difference in time when Dad's face was lit by the outside light and when it wasn't lit. And then people took the place of—but it's very confused."

Her slow delivery of this startlingly clear picture of a minor stroke was unlike anything the doctors with their clipboards and questions had managed to elicit.

She underwent a CAT scan, and afterwards the chief

doctor said it showed some vascular changes indicative of a number of mini-mini strokes over time, but nothing that explained what was happening now, no bleed in the brain. "I don't have anything I can treat. Sometimes a mini stroke can get better in twenty-four hours." The blood thinner was at the right level.

My mother came home the next day. The residence doctor dropped by in the afternoon, sturdy, energetic, reassuring. We had learned he was from Aberdeen, a fact that only endeared him further to my parents, for the Hays traced their origins back to the same part of Scotland. My mother greeted him cheerfully, and he said, "So you've come back."

She had. She had come back to us.

Then once again, around the middle of March, she lost her words and twenty-four hours later showed no signs of recovering them. "I'm thinking—throne—thinking—th." Starting on a word with an opening sound like "th," she could not escape it, any more than a month earlier she had been able to escape "window—whether."

After I got her lying down, I went into the living room to talk to Dad, who was staring out one of the windows that overlooked the road and the canal beyond. Without turning, he said, "I don't think she's suffering, she's just lost." He choked up, as he did so very easily, before going on. "We just have to hope, or maybe hope is the wrong word. If she doesn't make it, maybe it's for the best."

The next day, "It's snowing snowing snowing snowing," she said, as we sat on a bench in the glowing sunshine.

Certain words were no problem for her: *yes, okay, right, super, thank you, well, son of a gun, really.* Over the telephone, I told Sochi about the automatic responses that still issued loud and clear from her grandmother. Sochi laughed and remarked that they were all affirmatives; someone else's might have been *shit*, *goddammit* and *fuck*. My mother's "son of a gun" was as close as she came to an expletive and it was always said with good humour.

Then the next morning, when I walked out of the late-winter sunshine into their living room, exclaiming what a beautiful day it was, my mother stopped me in my tracks by replying from the chesterfield, "Yes, it is a beautiful day."

Lazarus was back from the land of the mute. Open in her lap was the book I had brought to them several days before about Shackleton's Antarctic expedition, and now she said how interesting she thought it was. Sitting beside her, washed over by relief and excitement, I flipped to the page with the photograph of ice flowers, delicate white rosettes blanketing the surface of newly frozen seawater on February 16th, 1915— four years before she and my father were born. I told her about seeing them in patches on the canal last winter and on a pond at the arboretum. And we made conversation. "Your words have come back!" She nodded and smiled and talked, and everything she said made sense.

But Dad was less excited by her recovery than he was upset with her for having wet the bed. "And who is going to wash the sheets?" he wanted to know. I asked him what happened to the diaper I had helped her into before leaving the night before. Well, in getting her into her nightgown, he had taken it off. Then immediately on the offensive again, he lit into me about her bone-strengthening medication. Had she had it or not?

"A nurse is supposed to give it to her early Sunday morning," I said, "which is today."

"You haven't answered my question!" he thundered, only to back off a heartbeat later. "All right," he admitted. "Somebody came in and gave it to her." Only to blast me again, "But then she fell asleep! She's not supposed to fall asleep after she gets it!"

He took things hard and he made them harder. There would come a day when he declared that the nursing care in this place wasn't "worth coon shit."

I liked "coon shit." Never in a million years would I have imagined those words coming out of his mouth.

We went down for coffee, and then Mom and I went outside into the open air and abundant sunshine while he remained behind in the library reading *Maclean's*.

In the flooding light we walked to the corner. "Did you have wrens nesting in the garden in London last spring?" I asked her.

"I am forced to confess that I do not remember," she said, speaking in her old formal way. Her teachers at Renfrew Collegiate had been sticklers for grammar and well-formed sentences, and my mother had been an excellent student.

"What was it like for you, the last couple of days, when you couldn't find your words?"

"It was unsettling. But it's been unsettling for a while."

We walked on. I asked her what she was thinking about.

"I'm thinking about what the future holds."

"Are you worried about that?"

She said something vague about no one knowing what the future holds, or perhaps I said that.

I had pulled from the wastebasket in their rooms another of her efforts at a letter, one she had been working on some days before, wanting it, she said, to be "a reasonable letter from a reasonable person." She intended to have it do yeoman's service for all of the friends she hadn't yet written to.

There must be a way in the English Landwich to say to
your English speaking friends a great deal more emphatic?
I've tried many ways but the best I've managed is

> *Thank you so very much from all of us*
> *The Hays*

Around this time, I remember her taking several bananas—
the three on the counter and the one from inside their little
fridge—and lining them up on the seat of her walker, then
pushing her walker into the living room. I didn't follow for a
moment, washing dishes in their kitchenette. Then when I
went into the living room, the bananas were nowhere in sight.
"Where are they, Mom? Dad, did you see what Mom did with
the bananas?"

"Sure I did."

"Where are they?" Looking around.

"Well, just don't sit on the chesterfield," he said.

I checked under the cushions and there they were: four
bananas lined up in a row.

They reminded me of characters out of Beckett. A pair of
solitaries who had always headed out to the studio, in my
mother's case, or downstairs to his study, in my father's (each
to his own lair) were now sharing two rooms. They were like
the aged parents trapped in dustbins in *Endgame*. Like Laurel
and Hardy in another fine mess. Or like old Joshua Smallweed
in *Bleak House* throwing cushions at his imbecile wife.

"Oh the weather," my mother said to me, "the weather
now is the pits of wet roses." She had been reading in the
newspaper, she said, about a woman in her thirties "who came

down under the overburden of blankets and probably isn't going to live."

Her turns of phrase rather confirmed my view that poetry issues from the holes in our head, that whatever faculty produces the startling contractions and coinages and leaps in logic that we call poetry is also available on an unconscious and uncontrollable level to someone suffering dementia. One morning on the telephone, ever solicitous about my sleep, she asked, "How did you severe the night?" Blending the words "fare," "survive" and "persevere" so deftly that a lifetime of labour in the sleep mines got summoned up and summed up. "Dad's behind a shave," she added, "but I think he'll come to the phone."

Later, when I went over to see them, "Do you know what I had for breakfast?" she said to me.

"What?"

She leaned forward. "Too *much*."

But that was her sense of humour. Like her abundant hair, it was her lasting glory.

AND THEN WE CAME TO
CANADIAN HISTORY

I THINK BACK to the Easter weekend in 2006 when I made a guilt-induced journey to London to see them. We went as a family, Mark and I and the kids. The snow got flatter and dirtier as we travelled west, until on the outskirts of Toronto low banks of grey and gritty foam edged the highway, a shrunken sight not unlike a dog left behind by his family, or the elderly in the last chapter of their lives.

My father looked like an old gardener. He had on his patched trousers and faded flannel shirt tucked in neatly, his cracked moccasins, and the dark-blue beanie he wore day and night to keep his bald pate warm. Outside, he exchanged the beanie for a bright orange tuque that came down in woollen folds over his ears and spiralled upwards into a sort of turban. His cloth jacket, pocket-filled and lined, came to his hips and was not a proper winter coat at all. He did not have winter boots; he wore old running shoes instead. No winter tires for his car either. "I've *never* had winter tires." For his hands, pockets rather than gloves.

My mother stayed inside when we went for a walk, her footwork too unreliable for anything but the driest road. My father's pace had slowed considerably. "I can't walk as fast as you do," he warned me. "You'll have to slow down."

We did not venture off the road, which led in a slight rise to the settled subdivision that was ideal for an elderly walk, being paved, snow-ploughed, level. No one else was out except for a middle-aged woman with a rosy-cheeked toddler in tow. She greeted us with a good morning and my father replied in his carrying voice, "You have your hands full."

"Boys love puddles," she smiled.

I saw us walking along, my father's head like an orange ice cream cone, a Dairy Queen to be precise, and it filled me with quiet, satisfied joy that we could be so unembarrassed together, parent and child. Embarrassment was a thing of the past. Although that very morning, before getting up, Mark had let out a sharp moan and pulled the blanket over his head. "What's wrong?" "Oh," he muttered, "I just remembered something from a long time ago that I'm ashamed of."

More accurate to say that sometimes, in peaceful moments, in forgetful moments, embarrassment seems a thing of the past.

Sunday morning we were at the dining room table, all but my mother, who was in the kitchen constructing our coffee. She wore the same clothes she would wear all weekend, pants with an elastic waistband that were easy to pull on, a blouse, a sweater, an oversized blue fleece jacket that came from who knows where. My parents did not shop for clothes. They wore what they had, wearing things out, casting off; a pair of old trees shedding their leaves for the last time. That weekend they passed on to us two more of my mother's paintings, a set of green china wash basins and matching water jug that had been Gracie and Conran's, a finely embroidered tablecloth and, prized possession, the antique embroidered sampler that came from my mother's mother's side of the family in Scotland.

"We are denuding your walls," I said.

"We have more stuff than we know what to do with," my father replied. "It's coming out of our ears."

I say "constructed" our coffee. My mother's coffee maker

had no glass carafe, so she used a laboratory beaker to catch the flow. It was a matter of carefully measuring the precious coffee and the water, making sure the beaker did not brim over, then pouring the coffee into mugs and heating them to scalding point in the microwave: an intricate routine that required her to be on her toes first thing in the morning. Others in search of the same early-morning stimulus will do the crossword or take a shower.

She joined us, making careful, crooked progress around the kitchen counter and into the dining room, her face alight with the gaiety that Yeats wrote about in a late poem as "ancient, glittering eyes." Between my parents there was much joshing and mutual insult. My father, more talkative than in the past, had discovered a way, it seemed, to be humorously, boastfully, insultingly loving.

I didn't know then what I understood later, that their gaiety came not from their lives together but from deep happiness at being visited. It wasn't that my father had actually become relaxed and talkative and loving in his old age. He was loving and talkative and relaxed on that weekend because we had come to see them.

And by that I don't mean they wanted us underfoot or next door. They wanted it to occur to us as a loving matter of course to visit them more often. I remember him once quoting something his own father was given to saying: that for his children the longest road out was the shortest road home. I took it to mean that no matter where his children were, they would always make sure their route included a visit home. A meaning tinged with sadness, because it wasn't true. My father had attended faithfully to his parents, but his brother and sister had taken off permanently to distant parts. Now I see that I misunderstood that too. The adage is really saying that taking a roundabout road brings you home more quickly than going in a straight line. It has nothing to do with visiting old parents. (Even if the thought remains that my earlier interpretation was also my father's.)

As usual, I was fishing for information about the past in connection with something I was writing, so as we drank our coffee I asked them about chokecherry jelly, remarking that it must have required impressive amounts of sugar, chokecherries being so tart. Sugar must have been very cheap when they were young.

"It *was*," my mother agreed.

"And how was the jelly made?" I asked.

My father spoke from his end of the table. "In a cloth bag."

Having secured my attention, he continued. The chokecherries were picked in clusters, twigs and all, and picked by him, "Who else?" Then boiled, the bag full of fruit submerged in a big pot, after which it was hung up to drip.

I asked if he ate any as he picked. He did not, even though they would have been ripe by then and not so tart. "They were ripe when they were black," he said.

He had picked them for his mother, for Gracie, from the line of chokecherry trees along the laneway to their house in West Hill.

My questions led inevitably to the old berry routine between my parents. As a child my mother had picked wild raspberries, a hot and scratchy job, and never got a cent, as she never tired of saying, while my father had had a summer job with Alfie Greenwood, who was the coal man in winter, picking his acres of cultivated raspberries for a dollar a day. My father went on in life to cultivate his own exceptional raspberries that my mother was always urging him to cut back in favour of tomatoes. Tomatoes made her eyes dance with pleasure. The night before, she had served bowls of pre-served raspberries for dessert to everyone except herself. "I'm sick of raspberries. I picked raspberries when I was a girl and I never got a cent."

"She drives me nuts with her raspberries," my father said.

It must have been the talk about gregarious Gracie's chokecherry jelly that led to his next blunt gambit. He said, "Your mother has no friends."

I shifted my gaze from his end of the table to hers. Her response was a small show of amusement, a non-answer.

"She'll talk to men," he said, "but she has no time for women."

My mother laughed aloud, even more amused.

"Except for Nomie," he said, referring to a woman my mother was fond of. "There's Janice across the street. She could drop dead, your mother wouldn't care."

What was he getting at, I wondered. My mother wasn't looking for friends. She had more friends than he did, if it came to that. And I suspected it did. My father, who didn't cook and didn't make friends, relied on my mother to feed him and give him a social life.

I said to him, "You have to remember you're married to an artist."

"That's right!" my mother said. "Thank you. Do you know that book *I Married an Artist*? It was very good and very successful. You remember," she said to me, "because we went to see the author. We took the streetcar to her house and knocked on her door and she invited us in, which is more than I would ever do."

"When?" my father said.

"Well, it was after the war."

"How could Lizzie be with you? She wasn't born yet."

"Weren't you with me?" she said. I shook my head. "Well, I took the streetcar to the end of the line—"

"*What* line," my father said.

"The northern line."

"Hog Valley," he said.

"Yes. And then we got out and walked. Can you imagine? Knocking on somebody's door to say you loved their book and wanted to meet them?"

My father said, "It's like this. She talks wildly all day long. It's only morning, but she'll keep on all afternoon and into the night."

My mother laughed again, amused by him, amused by herself. "Do you know what he said to his mother when he was a little boy? They were in the kitchen—"

"It was at the gate," he said.

"This is *my* story. You were in the kitchen and you said to Gracie, 'You make me sick and tired, and you have been like this all day.'"

"I went to meet Father at the gate," he said, "to get the newspaper from him, and he asked me how Mother was, and I said, 'She's sick and tired, and she's been like that all day.'"

"I like my version better," my mother said.

Chokecherries were on my mind because I had started a novel about a schoolmate of my mother's who went out to gather them in the summer of 1937, carrying two kettles as containers to fill, and when they found her body at sunset, in the bush on the edge of town, one of the kettles was partially full and the other was empty.

Now I produced a big brown envelope and said, "These will interest you."

They were copies of examination papers passed on to me by a friend who regularly visited her mother in a nursing home and befriended others there, including the old gentleman who had kept his Latin, history, physiography, and English grammar and composition exams from 1934.

First, we marvelled at the grammar examination that began with an elaborate extract about political blindness and proceeded to require the pupils to *write in full each subordinate clause in the above extract and state its grammatical value and relation, then parse fully the underlined words.* I read aloud other questions that asked for examples of the present progressive and the past emphatic and the future promissive, none of which any of us knew, though my parents must have known once.

We turned to the Latin examination and read out the sentences to be translated, feeling centuries away from the literate and disciplined days of the 1930s.

For many hours the troops were defending themselves with swords.

Those messengers whom we have captured are Gauls.

We shall march as quickly as possible through their territories.

Our men have useful arms with them.

As all the ships had been smashed, the enemy were compelled to surrender.

I said, "That's Latin for you. Fight, fight, fight."

And then we came to Canadian history. *Explain the causes of the War of 1812 and the causes of the Red River Rebellion. Give two important consequences of each conflict.*

I closed my eyes. "Consequences of the Red River Rebellion: expansion of the West at the expense of the Indians, and Quebec went Liberal."

My father, the old history teacher, nodded. "Yes, after the Conservatives hanged Riel, Quebec went over to the Liberal Party."

I closed my eyes again and shook my head in fuzzy sorrow. "The War of 1812. I always get confused. The Americans invaded Canada and died in our snowdrifts. But why did they invade?"

My father said, "It had to do with the Napoleonic Wars."

I nodded and tried to pull the vague pieces into a coherent shape, but failed. Then my father confused me even more by saying, "It had to do with the American Civil War."

The American Civil War started nearly fifty years later, but none of us hurt my father by saying so. He said, "Irish sympathizers in the States would come into Canada."

"The Fenians," I said. "Who killed Thomas D'Arcy McGee."

My mother piped up. "Tell me about Thomas D'Arcy McGee."

"One of the Fathers of Confederation," said my father.

I nodded, for suddenly, on this seasick ocean of mislaid facts, I had spotted shore. "He came home after midnight and was shot in the back. I read about this last week. He was at a late-night session in the House of Commons delivering one of his rousing speeches in favour of Confederation. Then he walked the two blocks to his lodgings on Sparks Street and as he turned the key in the door a Fenian shot him in the back. Although some say it wasn't a Fenian at all."

"When was this?" my mother said.

"1867," my father said.

It was 1869, but I didn't correct him. I went on. "The following winter his murderer was hanged and that same day a blizzard blew up and snow fell every day for the next two months. It was the year of the famous snow. Thousands of people, who'd come in from the Valley for the hanging, never got home. They had to take shelter with strangers. In April it began to rain and melt, and there were tremendous floods in the Ottawa Valley."

"All because they went to a public hanging," my mother said.

"That's right." Both of us casting aside history for the spirit of the story.

"Where did they bury the hanged man?" she asked. "I want to know because I was in St. Thomas when they dug up corpses next to the jail. The archaeologist was very kind and let me draw his hands."

"Potter's field," I said. "That's where they buried paupers and unclaimed bodies in the past. Every cemetery had a potter's field."

She asked me why they called it that, so I went in search of a dictionary and returned with it to the table. I looked up "potter" and found the definition. "'A burial place for strangers. Matthew 27:7.'"

I then went to the same bookshelf in the living room and returned with the leather-bound Bible given to my father when he was a boy. I opened it to Matthew. Starting at the beginning of the chapter, I summarized as I went along. "They're leading Jesus away and delivering him to Pontius Pilate. And then Judas repents and brings back the thirty pieces of silver to the priests. And they say, 'What is this to us? See thou to that. And he cast down the pieces of silver in the temple, and departed, and went and hanged himself.'"

I looked up, amazed by the turn of events our morning had taken. "Happy Easter," I said in wonder.

It was Easter Sunday. We had gone from one hanging to another, from the last public hanging in the Ottawa jail to Judas hanging himself from a redbud tree two thousand years ago.

Looking down again at the page, I read even more slowly. "'And the chief priests took the silver pieces, and said, It is not lawful for to put them into the treasury, because it is the price of blood. And they took counsel, and bought with them the potter's field, to bury strangers in.'"

The meaning of a very old story had landed with a thud in our startled laps. Amidst the muddled and ungraspable, here was something still and clear. Our lives stretched in a taut line back to the moment that gave us the phrase "potter's field."

On our way home, after passing endless Toronto and reaching Belleville, we turned off Highway 401 and came to Madoc. I had been reading while Mark drove and now I glanced up at the twisty, turning, pretty little town where my mother came to study art one summer, and through which my parents always drove on their way to the cabin near Lanark. We were in another world. We were entering what for me is mythical eastern Ontario.

The rising and falling countryside drew us forward to my mother's birthplace in the Ottawa Valley, the land of wild raspberries and chokecherries and stories that stick in the mind. Once again I felt the tingling of an unbroken connection. I knew that the girl who went out to pick chokecherries lay buried in the cemetery in Renfrew. Near the grass-covered stone marker that bore her name stood a handsome headstone for the family of the young man suspected of killing her but acquitted for lack of evidence. After the trial, he left town and assumed a new name, but there on the headstone was his real name, listed with his siblings. In the same cemetery lay the remains of the high school principal who committed suicide several years later, the man my mother always suspected of twisted sexual urges dangerous for any girl within his reach. Even in the final year of her life, when her mind was in tatters, she would remember with razor-sharp clarity the way his eyes followed her as she walked the length of the school corridor, all alone.

At home, I researched a few things to remind myself for the umpteenth time of episodes and characters I would forget again, so elusive is the tracery of official Canadian history. Set against that tracery are the colour and weight of the stories that never leave us, when we till the fields of memory and turn up the bones of Judas.

HE WEPT

I LOOKED AROUND the retirement home and saw wartime. The battlefield was old age and these were the victims, rather nobly and philosophically coping with their injuries, or not. My favourites were a tall white-haired gentleman who had lost the ends of his fingers during the war but still managed to play the piano, and the feisty, dignified ninety-four-year-old woman who had been Diefenbaker's secretary in the last ten years of his life, after he was no longer prime minister. She belonged to a book club and shared my view of the novel they were reading. "I hate it," she said passionately. "It's all nonsense." I was also very taken with a retired professor, ninety-nine years old, who was still reading Milton.

Mark came back from paying a visit to my parents one morning and said how lucid my mother was, but very low. Why go on? What was the point? She thought of just not eating, but didn't think she could do it. She talked about her bed as "that place where I'm crippled and stupid," and said she wanted one of those Dutch passports you can swallow. He told her Jeannie was coming in April, you'll want to see her. And he encouraged her to take pleasure in small things.

I went to see them in the afternoon and she said, "I was blue. Then the day came along and revealed what was behind it all." I asked her to explain and she tried, but the morning's clarity was gone. "Well, the *Ottawa Citizen* published that this was the last day of—my tardy memory was not taking full value of the news, that the news was publishing the news that the government was going to be adding this nightingale—publishing the fact that the news, this morning's news, was putting up the paper that the partner on yesterday's cage—that the Ottawa Valley paper was published with the news of this new tax. Mark was very good because he put a new light on this new tax—the whole bloody business of the tax coming on a new day."

When suppertime got mentioned, she said, "Well, Daddy, do you think we have the energy to peel some potatoes?"

"Before it was apples," he said genially.

My mother went in and out of lucidity the way you go in and out of a lake. The lucid waters, the forgetful shore.

In the drawer of her desk I found a note to their neighbours in London, unsent and out of mind, her handwriting no longer minuscule, but bravely hoping to fill the page.

> *Dear Tom and Kyle—*
> *Good to hear from you both! Glad to get your news. Glad to have news of you and to know your latest news. We've managed (in a kind of way) to keep in touch tho' we haven't had as much time as we would have liked—*
> *The Days seem to have gotten shorter—Either that or there aren't as many minutes in the hour—Ah well—or whatever—Son of a gun—or as we used to say "Son of a dirty gun!"*
>
> *Much love from us both!*
> *Gord and Jean*

I mailed it. In its way it was a great letter.

———

One night in late March my father said to me, "We left it too late. We should have come sooner. I guess I was the obstacle."

I suggested the London studio was the obstacle. Mom would not leave her studio.

"And I wasn't interested in the studio," he said. "I tried to keep her out of the studio. That was my mistake."

Embracing his gloominess, he added, "It's going to get worse."

"We've managed to deal with things so far," I said, trying to believe my own words, "and we'll keep on managing."

But we were both worn out. The next day he dumped his worries in my lap, everything from Mom's glasses needing repair to her wetting the bed again to his banking to his Visa card: all this combined with my own obligations—a panel the following day, a trip to Hamilton the day after that, my French lesson, the broken car (in the shop, something wrong with the compression), my stalled manuscript—all this meant that I was in torment, awake at three in the morning, an agony of worries until four, when finally I got up and immediately felt better, as if worries gain perspective when they're stood upright on their own two feet. Otherwise, they are the hot iron and you the thin cotton being pressed flat.

Tenant insurance in the retirement residence was yet another saga, yet another bayonet charge into the tangled barbed wire fence of being old and living too long.

My father argued from his trench, and not without reason, "Why should we have insurance? We don't need insurance. We have nothing to insure. They have insurance on the building."

"But not the contents of each apartment," I said. "And then there's personal liability."

To my father (and to me) it was yet another expense in a ruinously expensive living arrangement, but the office manager had persuaded me that he should fill out the form and pay the $125 per year by citing the example of a tap left running that flooded the apartment below and caused thousands of dollars of damage.

"Why would I leave a tap running?" my father demanded.

"Forgetfulness," I said.

"I wouldn't leave a tap running," he said.

Mom's small voice came from the chesterfield. "I might."

I thought I had convinced him, but a week later I noticed the form on his desk—filled out by me, still unsigned by him—and asked about it. He said, "We don't need insurance." So I went through it all again with the result that he agreed to talk it over with the office manager. But then he got the flu. The next week the front desk handed me the form, which he had left in the bathroom across from the dining room. So I gave it to him, saying what it was.

"*That's* not the form," he erupted. "It didn't look like that. *That's* not the *form*."

A further rigmarole involving Revenue Canada and many phone calls, all of which he and I needed to make together, had him accusing me of taking things out of his hands. He said he was being "trodden under."

Then, "We don't need this silence," he said into the silence.

Then, "Your mother doesn't ever leave me alone. If I could only work at my desk in peace and quiet, but she comes and interrupts and wants to know what I'm doing. She can't work at her art anymore. She can't do anything anymore. I know she's my first job, but I don't have a moment's peace to be at my desk."

Mom was sitting in the middle of the chesterfield. She said, "Well, I am truly sorry about that."

Dad was in his green wing chair next to the window. "I'm not used to being so disorganized." A pause. "It's such a shame," he said.

"What did you say?" Mom said.

"It's such a *shame*."

He meant her mind, his mind too; their lives. Her lost hearing aid (likely thrown out in one of her cleanups). Everything.

I went to him and kissed his forehead and held his shoulders. He wept. "I hate you having to hold my hand," he said.

At home, working on my novel, I moved between the fictional and the real, shifting inside and among the characters and myself. In a loose sense I had taken my father and divided him in two in order to create the sympathetic teacher Connie Flood and the unbalanced principal Parley Burns. Dad was my Jekyll and Hyde, and also my mirror image. He was as attached to his desk as I was to mine, and our moods were equally dependent upon how Mom was doing.

One day in early April of 2009, I went over to give my mother her bath and found them both in good spirits. Dad said he thought she was much better. "Don't you think your mother is much better?" he asked halfway through my visit, pressing his hopeful point, and I agreed, even though she thought I had come in by train and when it was time to go down for dinner she asked if she needed her coat. Hardest for him was watching the fog roll back in. He said he couldn't understand why sometimes she seemed better, and he would think she was coming out of it, and then she would sink back in.

There was the day when I was telling them about forth-coming appointments, one with the bank, another with the doctor. At mention of the doctor, my mother said, "That's what I wanted to know! Write it down." So I took her to the calendar on the wall and pointed to where I had written it down. She looked and said, "It's clear on the calendar, but it's not clear in my head." Dejected, she went back to the chester-field. I sat down beside her and asked if there was some other way I could write it out for her. She closed her eyes. Then she reached over with her left hand and hit me twice on the shoulder, hard. "Stop looking at me!"

I switched to the armchair and picked up a section of the newspaper and began to read it, then looked over at her. Her eyes were still closed and there was such a look of mental pain—soul-pain—on her face. Her skin was grey and her fea-tures a little twisted. She stood up after a bit and went to the bag full of clean laundry and summer bedding. Then she went into the bedroom. I put the clean clothes away in the closet, then followed her into the bedroom. She was standing at Dad's desk, touching things. Immediately, she went back into the living room. Wherever I was, she was not. I removed the winter comforters from the duvet covers, spread thinner blanketing on the beds, stuffed the comforters onto shelves in the closet, checked and cleaned the bathroom a bit, then announced that it was time for me to go. Dad said, "But you just got here." He had been all this time reading the news-paper in his chair by the window.

Before leaving I wrote on a pad of paper *Thursday*, and under it, *10:30 a.m.* and the doctor's name. I gave the pad of paper to Mom. She held it, reached for a pair of scissors and proceeded to cut into the paper. She managed to cut out a small triangle, which she put on the table beside her. Digging into the paper with the points of the scissors. Not starting at the edge. Like a child with her first pair of scissors.

She followed me to the door and I hugged her and told her I loved her.

The next morning I went over in time for the doctor, ten minutes before he was due to arrive. Dad came to the door to greet me, vulnerability and welcome writ on his face. Alarmed, I asked if everything was all right. He said he was just glad to see me.

He actually said that. And more than once too. He even called me sweetheart one day. In fact, he was always glad to see me; it was sorting out whatever needed to be sorted out that plunged him into bad temper.

There was no sound from Mom, none of her usual words of welcome. She was in the armchair and stirred herself a little when I went to her. A depressed and absent little figure. Though more animated as we sat together. Then the doctor arrived and she lit up. He came in, brisk, genial, dressed as usual in dark trousers and a short-sleeved white shirt, speaking with a trace of Scottish accent. He would alter her blood pressure medication, pursue the geriatric assessment, book a dermatologist for her skin sores.

After he left, Dad said to her, "So what got decided?"

He proceeded to grill her, the old schoolteacher asking questions to which he knew the answers. My mother, frail and flattened back against the chair, struggled to answer, tormented. "A periatric," she said.

"All right," he said. "Geriatric."

She struggled for the word "assessment," and he provided that too.

"What did you hear about at breakfast," he continued, "that we then saw written up in the paper?"

It was intolerable, what he was doing, but I did not cut him off.

She thought and thought, cornered, pressed. Then answered something about Liz being held in a building, and this wasn't right, she said, it was just something in her head, after fishing around and elaborating a scenario of me in a building somewhere and getting out of the building.

Dad said to me, "This bears no relation to anything." He picked up the newspaper and pointed to the story about the diplomat Robert Fowler, finally released by his North African kidnappers. In fact, it bore quite a resemblance.

My father was given to this. It was his cruellest habit, interrogating her like a sadistic headmaster in order to reassure himself that his mind was the more coherent. How I wish I had put a stop to it. Instead, I sat tongue-tied, at best coming to my mother's defence by telling her, jokingly, not to put up with it. But never did I address him: "Dad, don't. It makes her feel even worse." I was a child who knew her place. I was a coward.

He was afraid too. I knew that. His fear about her mind and his mind and what the future held made him overreact, made him lash out. There came a day when he raised his hand to a nurse. Going into the dining room, he wanted to know where his pills were. She asked what pills, did he mean his eye drops? (My father handled his own pills but the nurses put in his eye drops.) He raised his hand and in his abusive voice said whatever he said. I can't remember. I apologized to the nurse, who said she had seen worse. Patients who spit their pills all over her, patients who kicked. She showed me a huge bruise on her leg. "That one really connected," she said.

Then there was his treatment of the serving staff. "More coffee?" one of them asked at breakfast.

"Well, what the hell do you think?"

I had to thank the poor young man, reassure him, say how appreciated the coffee was, etc., etc.

Let me hasten to add that my father could also be gracious—his mother's son, a man with impeccable manners. When they first moved into the home, his charm got a real workout with the director of care. A woman in her late thirties from Newfoundland, she had the accent, the warmth, the style and humour typical of that less inhibited and more garrulous part of the country. She and my father got along like a house on fire. She flattered and teased him, and he came alive in her presence with quips and smiles and appreciation. So this is how you worked your wiles, I thought, as I watched him flirt shamelessly. This is how you had your school secretaries eating out of the palm of your hand. Then a month and a half into their sojourn as inmates—I will use his word—came the wretched news that she would be leaving, to be replaced, grimly, by a Mrs. Blood.

My father was in his wing chair when I gave him the news. Utter disgust darkened his face as he shook out his newspaper, saying, "It's a *revolting* development. No one can replace her. That personality is unique."

I had to smile at his use of the word "revolting." He tempered nothing.

One afternoon in May, I arrived at their rooms to see an Arctic painting of my mother's taken down off the wall and placed on her worktable. My father was trying to get her to paint it over. He had the original photo of Young Al Fishing in his hands, the three-by-three-inch black-and-white snapshot. "I think she should take this photo and paint it on this canvas. I've drawn in where I think Al should be and she can do the rest. She needs something to do! I want her to work on something—tinker and fiddle with it."

Mom smiled and laughed and said it was a good idea. She was humouring the testy, driven teacher.

Later, by ourselves in the courtyard garden, I asked her if she was all right with what he was doing to her painting.

"*No!* But he needs something to do. It doesn't matter. Really, it doesn't matter. The painting can be painted over. It doesn't matter a *hoot*."

Then, a bit later, "I want it to be over."

"Your life?"

"Yes."

Yet we were very content to be sitting side by side on the bench beside the pool of water with the little waterfall. A warm day and she looked surpassingly beautiful. She had on lipstick and was wearing blue.

The Arctic painting went back on the wall. Dad's pencil marks were easily erased. Something did get painted, however. I arrived one day in June to find my mother stretched out on the chesterfield. Though she maintained she was fine, Dad said she was having trouble getting up and down, and he had called the nurses.

Ever alert to the return of infection, I rolled up her pant leg to check on her knee, and to my amazement her leg was painted yellow. I rolled up her other pant leg. Yellow, all the way up her shin and into and over the lesion that never healed.

I said to her, and I know my eyes were wide, "You're not to paint your legs."

She looked taken aback. "I'm not?"

The trail of yellow was on her hands, on her upper lip, on

the arm of the chesterfield and on the carpet. It led to her worktable, to the canvas I had bought in February that she had covered in white paint, then set aside. It was yellow too.

I worked fast, washing her legs with soap before the nurses came, managing to remove all the paint except for some remaining in the lesion. I didn't want them to think that she had gone completely off her rocker.

After I got home, two strong memories came back to me. I remembered my brothers playing cowboys and Indians, and how my artistic mother would daub their cheeks and foreheads with streaks of paint, fashion headbands for them, insert feathers, then embellish the whole effect by painting horses on their bare chests. And I remembered something central to my own life that even fifty years later was never far below the surface.

MY LEGS

I WAS THIRTEEN when my mother had a quiet word with me in the kitchen. She said she and my father wanted to speak to me privately.

We were living in the small town of Mitchell then, in a new bungalow beside the highway leading into town. At the bottom of the field behind our house flowed Whirl Creek, which joined the Thames River in the middle of town. Across the road was a dairy farm and next to it a cemetery. I used to set off to school as trucks whizzed by and imagine them slamming into my guts. We had moved from Wiarton three years earlier, leaving that story-filled place on Georgian Bay for this small, conservative, inland town where none of us was happy.

It was after supper and the dishes were done. I followed my parents outside to our station wagon parked in the gravel driveway and got into the back seat. My mother slid in beside my father and he drove us to the other side of town, to the high school where he was the principal and I was in Grade Nine.

I don't recall if I guessed what all this was about. I know I didn't ask. I held my alarm to my chest. My parents would tell me my transgression when they decided to. It was early spring, as I remember it. I had already endured six months or more in my father's school. There was no snow on the ground, of that I'm sure. We parked in the paved lot reserved for teachers. A separate parking lot on the other side of the one-level red-brick school, recently built, was for the vehicles owned by any students lucky enough to have one. My father's ambition had brought us here, to Mitchell, his desire to move up in the world and run a larger and better school, but something I had done had brought us to this moment.

We got out of the car and walked across the lot to the school's side door, which my father unlocked. Then he led the way down the long corridor lined on either side with metal lockers the colour of well-chewed gum. The floor was polished and shiny. An immaculate school. My father would have stood for nothing less. Down the hall we went, our footsteps echoing, until we reached the main corridor and turned left. Just beyond the glass-fronted cabinet of sports trophies on one side and the secretary's office on the other was the principal's office. My father opened its door and we followed him inside.

In Wiarton his office had been smaller. At first it was only a roll-top desk in a walled-off corner of a classroom. Then after an extension was added to the original limestone building, he had his own office with a more substantial desk and a chair that enchanted me by rolling back and forth on coaster wheels. In Mitchell what you saw as you entered his office was a big plate-glass window overlooking the grassy courtyard and in front of the window a wide desk that rivalled John F. Kennedy's, in my estimation. Positioning himself behind it, my father stood for a moment looking down at the felt blotter on its surface. By now my mother and I had seated ourselves in the two straight-backed chairs facing his desk. My father lowered himself into his swivel chair.

What had I done?

He gave me a long, unflinching look. "Your mother," he

said in that deep bass voice of his, "has informed me that you are shaving your legs."

It's not hard to tell this story and get a laugh. I have from time to time. But now that I am considerably older than my parents were then, the three of us break my heart a little. They were in their mid-forties, puritanical, strict, but not without theatrical flair, you have to admit. In the evening light, in the dead quiet of his office, we were like actors on a minimalist stage set. One drawer of his desk contained the strap freely used in those days, though there was no danger of my being strapped. The setting itself did the work.

I say there was no danger of my being strapped. I knew that my father had strapped my brother Al for having raised some sort of ruckus in a classroom. But physical punishment for me had ended once I began to menstruate and wear a brassiere.

Why, my father wanted to know, had I shaved my legs when my mother had told me not to do so until I was sixteen?

I stammered out an inane and disingenuous answer. I did not say that I knew I was breaking the rules but it was excruciating to have hairy legs in gym class. Or that I was already a misfit by virtue of being his daughter. Or that there was no harm in it, there really wasn't. I didn't put up any sort of argument. I said, "I saw the dark hairs coming out of my legs and they were ugly and so I shaved them off." As if the hairs were so many mosquitoes I was swatting away. What else was a person to do?

I had used the razor in the medicine cabinet while taking my Saturday-night bath, leaving telltale hairs on the white inner rim of the bathtub. I had been careless. Or else I was practising a defiant, self-defeating, sneaky sort of honesty.

From behind his desk, my father said, "You'll wait until you're sixteen."

My mother, his reliable second, was silent beside me.

His expression yielded then. "We don't want to lose you," he added, as if that were the real point.

I understood. He meant that I might turn into a bad girl. He meant they loved me.

Afterwards, in the parking lot, we waited for him as he went to retrieve a piece of litter blowing about at the edge of the field. I can feel the cool wind on my face, feel my mother's presence beside me, see my father as he reaches the fence and bends down to collect the piece of trash. I hear my mother say, her voice touched by awe, "He is such a good man."

She meant he was a man of few but wise words, who cared about his daughter and his school and the litter that thoughtless people tossed about. She was inviting me to share her view, to appreciate him as she did.

He walked back to us, holding the potato chip bag, or whatever it was, between his bare fingers, the long wisps of combed-over hair lifting off his scalp in the evening breeze, and I recall exactly what was going through my mind. The relief that it hadn't been worse. The awareness that I had been taken back under his taciturn, demanding, unfashionable wing. The knowledge that my life was going to be harder now in a very basic, visible way.

It's something only girls, and maybe only certain girls, fully understand, the loss that comes with puberty. We lose our slim, smooth, unselfconscious bodies. We find ourselves overtaken by flesh and body hair, by sexual excitement and acute embarrassment. What a drama. What a before-and-after, this business of being physically happy and at home in the world, and then not.

I think back on myself, bemused that underhandedly

shaving my legs was about the extent of my rebelliousness. The Beatles had swept all before them, but in my bedside drawer I kept a picture of Elvis torn from a magazine, the still slender Elvis of *Fun in Acapulco*. Like my father, I was stubbornly behind, or outside, the times.

In that staunchly conservative town, he voted Liberal. He thought that Kennedy's poor judgment was to blame for the Cuban missile crisis. He did not believe in war, and only spoke of his wartime service in the Canadian Army to make jokes at his own expense. He had no time for the Legion. He didn't care for the pieties trotted out every Remembrance Day. He spoke to school assemblies about Albert Schweitzer's self-sacrifice and reverence for life. At exam time, he used to drive my older brothers and me to school on Saturday morning and put each of us in a separate classroom to study. In some countries there is no separation between religion and state. In the country of my growing up, there was no separation between home and school. No escape.

And then, in one of those narrative turns that reshape a life, there was. At the end of Grade Ten came the astonishing rescue at the hands of this same man, when he moved us to England for a year and the world opened up in ways I had only dreamed of. Around me were double-decker buses and every English accent I could have wished for. Ahead was a year of concert halls and palaces and parks, of grammar school and train rides through the British countryside. The following summer we travelled by car through Germany, Switzerland, Spain, Italy. I was fifteen by then. One afternoon in Florence, in our hotel room, I took a dry razor to my bare leg in front of everyone. Stu watched open-mouthed. "How do you do that?" he said. "Doesn't it hurt?"

The look on my mother's averted face was surprisingly tolerant. Perhaps my father was elsewhere. In any case, nothing was said. I shaved away, determined, liberated.

In that same hotel room a previous traveller had left behind on the chest of drawers two paperbacks by Hemingway. The magic of the old Penguins. I pounced on them and read them during those several days of sightseeing. On the day we left, I put them back on the chest of drawers. "You should have them," my mother said to me. "Take them." Her permission dazzled me. They were the first books of my very own, that is to say, not borrowed from a public library. I still have them. My name is on the flyleaf in pencil, and the place and date. *1967. Florence.*

The pocket size and weight of them, the soft, thumbed feel of the paper, the clean look of the typed sentences going evenly down the page, the intimate, dusty smell that came off the paper. They pulled me forward into the life I wanted, a world in which books and writing would sweep me up and take me somewhere far beyond myself.

Two years later I left home for university. After that my parents accepted whatever I did without comment. They handed over the reins entirely. And they never lost me. I always stayed in touch. I never went to the bad.

For a long time I was intrigued by the tragicomedy of my shaved legs for the light it shed on me. Now what interests me is the light it sheds on my parents. I understand why my father had to don the armour of his office before he could talk to me. He was an overbearing man, but he was also a shy man whose desk did much of his talking for him. My desk is my refuge too. I like to be alone in a quiet room with paper and pencils, working on a story like this one about my father having to deal with a daughter with whom he shared apparently nothing. Yet he was the one who paused and looked down at me when I was twelve or thirteen, curled up as usual with a book, and offered the radical thought, "You read so much. Have you ever thought of writing?"

Maybe my parents told themselves they were sparing me embarrassment by staging that conversation not at home but in a neutral place, as if my father's office were a neutral place, as if that inquisition were a conversation. They could have talked to me in my room, but they decided to make an impression. Maybe they wanted to throw their weight around. Maybe they were as deeply embarrassed as I was. Probably they were. And maybe they had lost their common sense in worry. In time I would learn that when our children worry us, our earliest insecurities mushroom all over again and cause us to overreact on a grand scale.

So out of their formal stiffness and awkwardness, their worry, a scene took shape. I don't suppose they set out to be theatrical, but drama ensued. Formality imposes on awkward people its own theatrical flair. It has us taking centre stage in an office or in a classroom or on the page.

There is one thing I know for certain. I felt tied to them afterwards in the difficult way one does—wanting to be the daughter they wanted, yet not wanting that at all. Tied to them, for good and ill.

JET IN ENGLAND

"IT'S TOO BAD," I said. "You were ready to leave much earlier."

"You're blaming me again," Mark said.

"Of course I am."

It was March of 2007. My parents were still in London, Ontario, and Mark and I were in the other London, late for dinner, pressing forward on foot on Willesden Lane, our eyes not nearly as sharp as our tongues. In the darkness we could not make out the numbers on the houses set back off the curving road, which was no lane at all but a roaring thoroughfare in a part of the city called Kilburn. The thickly attractive murkiness of the scene felt familiar to me from having lived here as a girl, when certain things about England went to my heart, among them early nightfall and the dingy brick walls that outlined gardens and swept along beside sidewalks, curving with them, so that you were guided away from certain things and toward others. In the distance an orangey-yellow glow indicated neon and we hurried on.

Running late made me vulnerable and aggressive. I harried myself with the image of our friends waiting for us in the Indian restaurant and hoped they would have the wits to go ahead and order. Otherwise, we would have to gobble a few samosas before rushing on to the theatre in time for the Pinter play; in time, no doubt, for two hours of grimness. My punctual father was on my mind, punctuality being as much a family trait as stubbornness. My son had said to me recently that my side of the family could be quite stubborn in a stupid way and not stubborn enough when it counted. A true observation if ever there was one. My truculent father was also a pushover, eager to be liked, socially insecure. His long-time financial adviser, a man he liked to call Gleever Gliver Glover, had shown up at their door one day, asking if he could use $100,000 of the money they had invested with him—all hard-earned savings—for some particular purpose he had in mind (bailing out his company, in fact) and without a single question my father gave his ready assent. Only my mother, who related the events to me years later after G.G.G. had lost the whole amount, only she raised a doubting voice. "Boyd, what do you need the money for?"

As it turned out, our friends, Duncan and Cathy, were late too, and they had indeed had the wits to order. We joined them at an undersized table soon laden with fragrant and mysterious dishes and I was talking too much.

I wonder why that happens. It's not just nervousness, it seems to me, but the wish to impress. And not just the wish to impress, but happiness and relief. I rattled on about all the plays and museums and galleries we had been going to, a non-stop recounting that included telling them I had lived here for a year when I was fifteen and explaining how it came about. My father had been taking courses every summer in Toronto with the idea of getting his master's degree in education, doing it bit by bit, until he met a man who had done it all in a year by enrolling in the Associates Course at the University of London. Dad came home and announced to my mother that that's what we were going to do. "We'll move to England for a year," he said. "But what about Jet?" my mother said.

I broke off. Without intending to or knowing where I

was headed, I had arrived at the heart of the matter so abruptly that I had actually brought myself to a stop.

This is one way stories get told. Under force of uncomfortable circumstances, you begin to talk and get carried away, only to arrive at the under-story, the unexpected underlying story, and your feet hit ground, real ground, and you pause.

My mother didn't say, "What about me? What about the children?" She said, "What about Jet?" Our beloved dog, at the time nine years old.

"This isn't going to have a happy ending," Duncan said, grimacing in sympathy and laughing with me. Cathy's face was responsive too. I could see she liked dogs or had some experience in this troubled line.

"It might have happened anyway," I began again.

We left Jet with the couple who moved into our bungalow in Mitchell. We knew them. My father had hired the young man to teach at his school. The young man and his bride agreed to look after our dog until we got back. But in the year we were away, Jet grew sick and old, and within seven or eight months of our return he was dead.

"We broke his heart," I said.

The voice of my editor in Toronto came back to me. My heart broke for him, she had said of someone we both knew. A word that sounds exactly as it should, like a snapped twig.

We had imagined his welcome. Imagined pulling into the driveway, piling out of the car to be met by a dog who leapt up on us, delirious with joy. In our vanity we had expected a show of undiluted devotion. But Jet came to us very slowly from behind the house, a grey old dog, and the only person he greeted was my father. With visible effort he lifted himself a few inches off the ground in an aged display of recognition and loyalty. The rest of us fell upon him, reassuring him how glad we were to see him, reassuring ourselves that he remembered us. Then we drew back disappointed, and fell away.

English darkness has a different look—sootier, older, filthier, richer-toned. You can breathe more easily in Canada. An American friend, a painter, told me how impressed he was by the black in the Canadian paintings at the National Gallery, different in tone from any other black he had seen. Not a hot Spanish black, or a northern European black either. He didn't know how to describe it.

I think of it as fresh. Jet's fur was jet-black and unusually soft for a Lab. He came to us as a pup from the butcher in Wiarton. He had a name, Velvet, which my brothers rapidly changed to Jet. I can see their four bare legs intertwined with his four furred ones as they skidded the length of the living room floor in riotous displays of boyish and doggy high spirits. His Lab fur was softened by some other breed, but he still had the fine blunt head of a Lab. He was a great favourite of Auntie Beth's whenever she came to visit, Auntie Beth whose liveliness also turned grim, but in another way.

Jet became the centre of our family, the one subject upon which we all agreed. He liked to stretch out in the doorway between kitchen and dining room, and we would step over him, sometimes reaching down to pat, sometimes stroking him with a foot, but never asking him to leave his place in the middle of our lives because it would have hurt his pride. He followed us to school. He brought chickens home to my mother. Failing chickens: muskrats. He fought pitched battles with any dog that trespassed on our property.

He lay under my sister's baby carriage whenever my mother set her outside for her nap and never left his self-assigned post. One night my father, passing through the living room, caught sight of a tuxedoed Gregory Peck presenting an Oscar, and stopped to say, "Now there's a real man!" As if all the other movie stars were ninnies. In my father's estimation, Jet was a real dog.

Only to live his final year like Lear deposed. Consigned to the basement, tolerated at best by the young couple in our house. Then to be restored, but too late.

The day after our dinner in the Indian restaurant, still dwelling on memories of Jet's sad end, I searched for and found the flat we had lived in forty years before: 8 Belsize Park. It hadn't changed, or very little. Three steps led up to the white, pillared porch of a handsome three-storey townhouse across the street from St. Peter's Church. From the sidewalk, our second-floor flat seemed the same, inhabited now by the owner of the black shirt drying in the kitchen window. This was the flat where in the final cleaning (my parents so conscientious they left it even cleaner than when we arrived), my mother discovered a ten-pound note under a mattress and did not tell my father, fearing that in his terrible honesty he would make her hand it over to the landlord.

I recognized certain smells, though they were less savoury than in memory. At fifteen, after all, I was experiencing my first winter of things being chilled rather than frozen, winter in England being less a season that shuts the door than a cool room with an open window. Our bathroom window remained ajar no matter the month. Across the sill came old-city smells of muted vegetation that passed over the bar of soap and the white-and-black floor tiles, rinsing the air inside and making it as complex as perfume or wine.

Having found our flat, I then retraced part of my way to school. I walked toward the street called Haverstock Hill and felt not so much in my feet as in my knees the rising of panic, slight but unmistakable. The sidewalk gave a heave as it rose steeply in the last section, more hill than slope, and there I was on Haverstock Hill, my Tube stop half a block away and me knee-deep in memories of being over my head—the terror of school lightened by the incredible fact of London, all so new, different, huge for a girl from small-town Ontario. The excitement so much bigger than the dread and the dread bigger than any I had known, as my young self made the trek to a grammar school in Camden Town, stoical, sloppy-in-the-guts with fear, while around me everything was so overpowering I could barely take it in. The reek of carcasses hanging in the butcher shop windows, the smell of flowering hedges and another kind of fuel—petrol, and not just the thickness of the air, not just familiar smells multiplied, but new smells in a new climate in a new place. And I understood why my parents had wanted Jet to stay in our house, in a place he knew, the air full of scents he had sniffed and parsed innumerable times.

Forty years. The time seemed as nothing until I got back to our flat near Russell Square, went to wash my hands, and caught my face in the mirror. I had aged as much as Pussy Galore. Her face, in the newspaper only a few days before, had been no less washed out, the colour of hay in a winter field, a loss of resolution in her features. My panic-tossed face was merely old. A quilt used for years, exposed to light, will fade the same way.

The face of memory is less reliable than the knees. Mine would have been bare in those days, under the regulation dark green skirt. I finished washing my hands and made tea. You come to the end of a journey and drink tea, with nothing for company except your state of mind. My thoughts drifted to Auntie Beth, her yearly visit, her particular fondness for Jet. She lent spice to my childhood: a pretty, petite woman who grew plump, soft as a marshmallow, diabetic, then lost weight and prettiness with it. She was my mother's oldest friend and a woman unlucky in love, who nevertheless was always cracking jokes, telling stories. What a contrast she made to my quiet parents and how fascinating to watch them loosen up in her presence. She would take a late-afternoon nap, and when it was dinnertime my father would say to Jet, "Go and wake up Beth." Jet would get to his feet, pad over to the chesterfield and lick her face with long, loving, practised licks.

"That wonderful dog," she said to me years later in her nursing home in Toronto. She was alone in her room, except for what she called her inanimates, an array of stuffed animals, each with a name like Popsy or Mittens or Flossie. "He licked my face all over. Like a plate."

Her head lay flat on her pillow. She wasn't wearing one of the wigs she had taken to in middle age. Her own hair proved to be long and sparse. She still had her soft skin and pretty hands and honeyed tongue. "Darling," when I arrived, "this is my lucky day."

Then, "I've never forgiven your mother. She left that wonderful dog in the street."

An accusation so venomous it took my breath away. Nothing she could have said would have hurt my mother more. But Auntie Beth was shrewd and knew how to be lethal.

"She didn't leave him in the street," I protested. "We left him with the people who moved into our house. So he would be in the place he knew."

"Well, I'm glad to hear it," she said sourly.

I saw blame in all its facets—ugly, insidious, sugared, prolonged. Nourished when everything else is gone. Auntie Beth had few pleasures, but toward the end she had this one, of blaming my mother for having neglected her.

"We couldn't take him with us," I persisted. "Any dog entering England had to spend six months in quarantine."

She turned her head away from me and spoke to one of her inanimates, "Now don't you cross the street without me, you naughty girl." Lucid and cutthroat in her dotage.

I weigh different forms of ruthlessness: the ruthlessness that leaks from an unfulfilled life, the ruthlessness necessary to have a fulfilling life. London opened up the world for us: a new career for my father, a painting life for my mother, endless possibilities for me.

It was late August when we pulled into the driveway of our former house in Mitchell. The sun was hot on the gravel and the gravel was full of weeds. My father would have had my brothers pull them out if we had been living there still. We arrived bursting with excitement, only for our spirits to plummet to the ground, as if we had arrived at a longed-for lake only to find it too shallow for swimming. I make the comparison thinking of our countless family expeditions to Red Bay when Jet was as eager as we were to get to the water. At day's end, as we set off for home, he would run beside the car for several minutes, coursing along beside us, drying out, until my father braked to a stop and we opened the back door and in he surged, clambering over us, still damp and reeking of dog. We would stop again for ice cream. From each of us he received the heel of the cone. There was a gentleness to the way he ate, his long tongue coming out and slowly, luxuriously licking. My mother held on to the heel of her cone the longest, making the pleasure for both of them last and last.

The day Jet died, I was walking home from school to our rented house on Oriole Crescent in Guelph, when my father and mother drove by in the car, and catching sight of me, Dad pulled over. It was early spring. My father was in his green corduroy coat with the brown collar, my mother in her fawn-coloured suede jacket. I got into the back seat and there was Jet in the last moments of his life. Since Christmas he had become sicker and sicker with cancer of the blood. He sat half-slumped on the back seat, unable to hold up his head. A thin veil of mucus trailed from his mouth, which sagged open. His eyes were glazed and gone.

I had seen my parents lose their composure a few other times, seen my father mop his eyes with his handkerchief, but never bent over the wheel and sobbing as he was when he returned from carrying Jet in his arms into the vet's office. My mother sobbed beside him. It took a long moment for my father to get command of himself. And then he drove us home.

We were gone too long that year we were away.

I think of Neruda's great carefree poem about his dog. It's one of his odes to simple things, like tables, spoons, chairs, salt. Neruda and his dog roam the countryside together, his dog full of questions, Neruda with no answers; his dog offers him the tip of his nose as a gift, a message of love. But all I can wonder is who looked after him when Neruda was away from home.

The year we were in England, Jet made a daily trek across town to my father's school in the hope of finding us. So my parents were told after we returned. One of my mother's friends used to see him outside when she drove by our house, looking as forlorn, she said, as a cold-cellar carrot at the end of winter.

In the last year of her own life, my mother soothed herself when she couldn't sleep by thinking back to our wonderful dogs, as she called them, to dignified Jet and to Hamish, his talkative, excitable successor. In her own decrepitude, as the world and her wits abandoned her, she held on tight to their message of love.

SIBLINGS

IT WAS THE MIDDLE OF MAY of that first difficult year my parents were in Ottawa. Early one morning, before dawn, Mark and I made a thermos of coffee and drove over to the Fletcher Wildlife Garden on the other side of the canal to look for birds. We parked the car and stepped out into a green world emerging from darkness, then set off down the path into the leafy air. It felt like skipping school.

Two degrees Celsius at 5:30 a.m. We wore gloves, warm hats and coats, long johns under our pants. We went first to the Backyard Garden with its bird feeder and bench and its arranged and identified spring flowers and wild plants. The sight of clear labels next to every growing thing soothed me to the bottom of my soul; what a relief to learn things, be reminded, have the names at hand. We poured coffee from the thermos into our camping mugs and saw a cardinal, red-winged blackbirds, white-crowned sparrows, a nuthatch, two rabbits. Then on to the pond and more red-winged blackbirds and huge raggedy robins, and tree swallows with iridescent backs and ample soft-white bosoms, and on past blossoming apple trees, wild, and two that were pink and white entwined, an ancient graft, like a strawberry-and-vanilla ice cream cone, two scoops, and on through the ash woodlot (not yet decimated by the emerald ash borer).

My mother had been an avid birder all her life. I was thinking of her as we turned right and came to another few apple trees, pausing to make out a bird, half-hidden in the branchy depths, when suddenly it flew straight at our heads and we ducked. A Baltimore oriole. We followed the flame-orange arrow down to a stand of trees closer to the canal and there we saw yellow warblers too, flitting from branch to branch inside a world that could not have been more different from the stale confinement of a retirement home. Finally, to be outside as I should have been all these years, observing the migrating birds at dawn. To live more of our lives in nature—there's the answer to all of our troubles.

It was spring. Time was actually passing. We had celebrated my parents' sixty-sixth wedding anniversary the day before, bringing them home for a special dinner of roast beef and Yorkshire pudding. My mother stood alone for a moment by the kitchen window overlooking the garden with its bird-bath set in the middle of the nearest flowerbed. "There's a lot of activity in the water," she mused. "It must be the dark reflections of the clouds overhead."

They were two of the loveliest sentences I had ever heard. Clear, calm, simple. The presence of water and sky, the play between liquid and light, had restored my mother to herself.

But she could not keep the family straight. We got Al on the phone and she spoke to him, "How are you, son?" Then twice she came into the kitchen looking for Stu, who was in Montreal. She had lost track of where her sons were.

I told myself it was natural. This weakening and fading happened to every living thing. It wasn't sad to enter the retirement home, or tragic to see diminished lives still hobbling and limping along. It was the natural course of all things.

Yet for my mother and father, the course was a prolonged

unnatural twilight of being fed, monitored, medicated, driven mad with idleness, while their pockets were drained and their brains were assessed, all in the name of improving the quality of their final years. "I'm at the end of my life," my mother often repeated. "Why isn't there a way to just say goodbye and then you could get on with your life." It was disgraceful and irresponsible, she would say, to be spending so much money to keep her alive. "That money should go to you kids."

On the other hand, she said to me one day, "I waver. We should be dead. We should be dead."

"You waver?"

"Because it's so beautiful outside."

We managed to set their minds at rest about their income. Mark drew up a spreadsheet to show how much money came in every month from my father's good teacher's pension and from their various investments and savings.

But the complications of those days, and my dread that they would never end. There was a night in June when I could not sleep at all, and at two, putting on my light robe, I went out onto the back porch with a cup of hot milk. It was a warm night. Breezes and mosquitoes were active, the breezes on my face, the mosquitoes on my ankles and wrists. "I can't take looking after my parents anymore," I said to the open air. The words came unbidden. In my head I proceeded to write to my brothers and sister, saying, "I'm not all right." I asked them to time future visits with some of the many doctors' appointments, to share the burden with me.

Weeks passed. Al came in July. Beforehand, he sent an email asking if he could arrive at midnight; it was a matter of arranging more than one flight, though I don't remember where he was flying in from. I thought about this. I thought about him wrecking whatever chances I had for sleep and felt raked over with resentment and bitterness. I wrote back that I wasn't thrilled by the hour, in truth. Then I couldn't resist telling my parents that my brother had wanted to show up on my doorstep at midnight and I had said no.

Immediately, the air was awkward. My mother said, "I don't know what the temperature is like between you, but you didn't realize he was joking."

"He wasn't joking," I said. The old wound lay bare.

It was after his visit (he managed to find another flight and arrived at an earlier hour), some time in August, that I made my fatal mistake. I penned the email to my siblings that had been in my head since June. I laid out how hard things were and asked them not to make extra work for me when they came. Jeannie and Stu sent sympathetic replies that soothed me. Al wrote, "I suppose this is meant for me. I hope, having vented, that you feel better. Certainly, I feel worse, so you have accomplished that much at least."

I replied immediately, saying mine wasn't a personal attack, but a cry for help. He wrote back, "You are the one who is supposed to understand the meaning of words."

I telephoned him. His voice was icy and nothing I said made it less so. The effect was like swallowing caustic soda. My insides felt scraped and scalded. You read about something being so cold it burns. It was like that. Like being caught doing something unbelievably bad as a child and your insides go into shock.

He wasn't wrong. I wasn't wrong either. My email *had* been directed at him. It *was* a cry for help.

I showed Al's email to Mark, who said simply, "He feels guilty."

In fact, Al did a great deal for Mom and Dad. There was

no reason for him to feel guilty. No, that wasn't it. We were both far too touchy, that was the trouble, and we rubbed each other the wrong way.

I went out to a pub with three women friends and ranted about my long, infuriating relationship with my brother. One friend interrupted me. She had received a similar letter from the sister who was looking after their mother in her old age, and her reaction was, "Fuck off. You took it on. If you didn't want to do it, why did you take it on? We were in Vancouver. There was nothing we could do. And what it all boiled down to was that she felt unappreciated. That's all it was."

"Feeling unappreciated," I said, "isn't nothing."

But people are quick to make the same point, that the child looking after the parent is doing so because she wants to. If only it were that simple. I had a friend who was so distraught after paying her daily visit to her mother, long ridden with Alzheimer's, that she went through a stop sign and totalled her car. Yes, I volunteered to take it on, but there was never a moment when I didn't wish to be let off the hook.

August drew to a close and one morning Al called and his voice was normal again. The ice had gone out of the bay. He made arrangements with me to drive Dad to the family cabin and then he offered to take over my parents' finances, even flying in once a month to do the banking.

"If you and Dad would like that," he said, his voice tentative, kind. He wanted to help. He also wanted me to be less pushy, less in-the-right all the time. That's what his tone of voice was telling me. I half heard him, half understood. I hear him more clearly now.

I thought he must have been talking to Stu. My eventempered oldest brother, who had always had a calming influence in the family, must have spoken in my defence. Years later, after Mom's death, I learned from Al that it was she who made the repairs, our dementia-plagued but noble-hearted mother. She had asked about the trouble between him and me, and he had sputtered, "Well, I didn't start it!"

She said, "But you can stop it."

Here is my dying wish. That someone will come over at 4:30 a.m. and sit with me as the birds begin to sing and identify each one, so that I won't go to my grave not knowing. A pot of strong coffee on the stove; one of those Dutch passports in the final cup.

For the next two years Mark and I followed the passage of the seasons with binoculars in our hands. We went back to the Fletcher Wildlife Garden in the fall to see the birds on their way south. Many leaves were already down and I saw the greys of twigs and branches and rock, the very structure of things, and thought about my father's essential character: what brought him to the edge of tears. Public admiration moved him, and so did ability and skill. When a whole town, for instance, applauded someone's athletic prowess. We were talking one day about Reg Krueger, who had come from nearby Hanover, Dad remembered, to play with Wiarton's senior hockey team, the Redmen, in the days when crowds filled the local arena to cheer their team on. "Reg was Wiarton's best athlete," said Dad, and immediately there was that telltale reddening around his eyes and quiver of his full lips. Knowing he would be interested, I told him about Mark going into the cheese shop on Bank Street when it was in the process of closing, everything 20 per cent off, and finding the owner wearing a Bruins T-shirt. Mark, in the Red Sox cap he wore all summer, asked him why he was a Boston fan. "Two words," the owner said. "Bobby Orr."

My father's face took a step back; he had to swallow to control his emotion. (When angry, his face would take three steps forward.) I went on to recount how one summer, when we were camping in New Hampshire, the park ranger noticed our Ontario plates and said he had never realized how wide Ontario was until he drove from the border to Parry Sound in order to see the birthplace of Bobby Orr. "The best hockey player there ever was," he said.

Again: the tears under the surface that Dad's face had to swallow. We think tears are a matter of the eyes, but once the monster is loose it tramples all over the face and chokes the throat and even kicks open the door to the chest.

My parents loved sitting on our back porch in the sunshine and the freely moving air. The porch overlooked our rather wild garden that ran downhill to a grassy lane. My mother would say, "I'm in love with your garden. I'm very much in love with your garden. It's so peaceful and quiet." She was entranced, as always, by the birds—not just the songbirds but the crows flying home in waves—and she began one night to talk about the birds she was watering, and if they were going to open. After a moment I realized she meant the bird of paradise in the bouquet in their living room. Of the flocks of crows that passed her window early in the morning and at the end of the day, she referred to what she rather dazzled me by calling "their quick copulative appearance." On another day, when I mentioned coming upon a raucous murder of them in the neighbourhood, she leapt in. "Crows," she exclaimed. "I'll tell you about crows. The guttural sniped takeoffs on their old stomping grounds and they just surround you, thousands and thousands of them. I know exactly how many there are. There are 205 crows and their mates. So that's about five hundred."

Crows were a life force and a visual feast. They clarified her mind. Never once did she stare at a crow and not know what it was.

That autumn the young sugar maple next door progressed through deepening shades of yellow before settling on old gold. "What colour would you say the leaves of that maple are?" I asked her, pointing out the window and wondering if she still had access to some of her painter's vocabulary. "What kind of yellow?"

Dad said, "There's only one yellow. Yellow."

Mark suggested saffron. Mom mentioned lemon yellow. And Mark brought her a lemon from the kitchen counter and they looked out the window, comparing lemon yellow to the old gold of the tree.

On one of her good days, as my father called them, when nothing was amiss and she and I were peacefully alone in their living room, I asked her how she was. She stared at the wooden coffee table in front of us before she answered, "You can live too long. All the children are grown up, they're fine, they're doing well. All the potatoes are peeled. I had fulfilling work and I can't do it anymore. Not everyone feels this way, but this is how I feel. I'm telling you because you asked. This in-between filling-in is hard."

I was reminded again of Samuel Beckett: You can't go on; you go on.

I asked her how she thought Dad was doing. He was downstairs taking part in the regular beanbag-throwing contest at which he often came out the winner. (I had paused to watch him once, impressed by his graceful ability to throw an object with accuracy, reminded of his skill at lawn bowling, curling, horseshoes.) My mother took even longer to answer, saying finally that he enjoyed reading the newspaper every day. "We're not enraptured with this life," she said.

On her worktable were several of the small assemblages she had made decades ago by using up leftover materials, including certain watercolours she had deemed unsuccessful and cut up into pieces, plus unusual buttons and shells she had collected over the years. Framed in black boxes, these constructions of hers were like jewels against dark velvet. She had taken to bringing them down off the wall and readorning them with pieces of origami paper, or old lace that she had saved. She glued the paper and lace directly on the glass, colouring it further with pastels. Sometimes she had Dad take them out of their frames and then she glued things to the matting itself, or coloured on it, not quite like a child but not like an adult either.

She was still making stabs at Al's portrait, having commandeered a different photograph. This one showed him on his tricycle, head turned in a backward glance, irresistible grin on his face. She had Scotch-thistled it with pins from her pincushion, using them to outline his head and arms, then pencilled in the background and pencilled around his eyes, turning his face into a fairly ghastly mask. Recently, she had laid the photo on a small canvas and painted around it and through it. As she tangled with the picture, Dad took pleasure in describing her as "pugnacious and awkward all day."

She herself said, "I'm up a crick with that painting. I'm up a crick with seven outlets. I've explored four, which leaves three. So I'm pissed off."

She said she knew what she *wanted* to do. "Convey that patch of sunlight in a dark surround." That sunlight being Al.

When her ninety-first birthday rolled around in November, word about it travelled through the residence, as word about birthdays did, and that evening I witnessed women coming up to kiss her. One crept forward in her wheelchair and touched her arm and said she wanted to give her a birthday kiss; she brought herself close and kissed my mother on the side of her face. Her companion on a walker said now it's my turn. She came close and kissed my mother on the forehead and wished her a wonderful year.

My sister paid one of her welcome visits. While she was here I slept deeply and without aid. As soon as she landed after her long flight from Mexico, she took a cab directly to my parents', so in the evening I went to get her and walk her home. Seeing Jeannie was in some measure like meeting myself. She was taller, but our colouring was the same and so were our voices. My mother once described the three of us as dark-voiced women. Her relationship to my parents had always seemed simpler than mine, unmarked by ambivalence. She said to me once that growing up, contrary to me, she had always tried to be good. Whenever she visited, she brought her clarinet and practised in the spare bedroom down the hall from my study. The sounds took me back to the various times I had come home from university to hear her warming up by doing scales, then launching into whatever piece she was learning. After Jeannie herself left home, and my parents settled into their late middle age, the house in London became so quiet and cut off from the world that to bring in a newspaper, to buy it the day it came out, was a revolutionary act.

I found the three of them relaxed and merry together, my parents rejuvenated by my sister's presence. Mom and Dad stood holding hands as we left them, smiling, beaming. Mom blew us a kiss.

They always held hands, in a manner of speaking, when they entered the dining room for their meals. My mother would park her walker in the hallway, my father would grip her by the wrist—not the hand, the wrist—and in they would go, swaying and tottering, until they reached their table on the far side of the room. From a distance all anyone could see was a pair of unsteady ancients holding each other up. My father pulled out my mother's chair and settled her into place before going around to his side of the table. Only if you were beside them did you hear the names he called her. In a good mood, "Here comes creepin' Jesus," if she lagged behind. And she would laugh with mirth and so would I. Or he might say, "Come on, Torchy Peden." And I would learn that Torchy Peden was the famous six-day cyclist before the war. In a bad mood he called her dumbbell or stupid nit. In a worse mood— say she failed to give him her wrist, but gave him her hand instead—he swore at her.

She let none of this trouble her anymore.

There was a morning when my sister and Stu, who had also come to visit, were reminiscing about growing up. We were around my kitchen table, and Jeannie startled me by saying, "Dad was so *horrible* to you and Stu."

I stared at her in surprise. I felt exonerated, almost lit up—yet it shocked me. I didn't want to believe it; I still hoped it wasn't true.

I looked at Stu for his reaction. But he deflected: "What really rankled with me," he said, "was the way he treated Mom."

"But then she fought back," Jeannie said. "When she turned fifty, she fought back." She added, "It was very uncomfortable to watch."

The rest of us had left home by that time, but we were aware of it too. Instead of brooding in wounded silence after one of his vicious put-downs, usually some slam about her stupidity, Mom would fire back a retort in her own defence. My father hated being challenged and I never once heard him apologize, so the air between them could stay splintered for quite a while before they came around to each other again. On one of my visits home—I can't help smiling as I recollect this—he spent half an hour zealously vacuuming the hallway and living room while Mom and I sat talking together at the dining room table. The old Kirby got louder and louder as he drew nigh, until he flicked it off and stood like a boy waiting for a pat on the head. My mother ignored him and kept on talking. He switched on the Kirby and went back at it. She smiled, "Let him keep on. It's good for him." What he had done to trigger her cold shoulder I never learned, but some rancorous explosion of his had earned a wall of silence from her.

In the short family history Dad wrote in the early 1990s, which I typed up for him, he has this line: *In the fall of 1941, I met Jean Stevenson who soon became number one in my life and has been ever since.* Several years earlier, around 1986, he had made a more revealing remark when he was sitting alone with me one afternoon. "The more she blossoms," he had said ruefully, "the more I retreat." He paused, absorbing the magnitude of what he had just admitted, then added, "I haven't told her that."

I don't believe he ever did. I trust that he didn't.

In the retirement home, as I say, none of his caustic remarks got to her anymore. She seemed to operate on a different plane, more spirit than flesh. I asked her once if she was working on something, and she said, "My mind is a lot bigger than I am. There are bigger things in my mind than are available to me." Several times she expressed her gratitude at being free of the burden of making meals. So that was part of her newfound ease and should not be underestimated: the end of laborious food shopping, kitchen duties, housekeeping.

At the same time she remained a very physical being. Sometimes I would drop by and find the two of them sitting close on the chesterfield, holding hands, a hot date. Every so often she still perched herself on his knee, putting her arms around his neck, both of them almost smacking their lips with affection. There was the day the doctor wanted to examine Dad's bowel, so Dad followed him into their bedroom, but she called to him to come back. He stopped. "What?" "Come back," she said from the chesterfield. He came back sideways, like Charlie Chaplin, to get a laugh, and she kissed her fingers and gave his rear end a loving pat.

On Christmas Day of 2010, nearly two years after their move from London, we were all gathered around my dining room table, all of us except Jeannie in Mexico. After the turkey, after the steamed pudding, my father stood up from his place at the far end of the table. He said he wanted to thank Liz and Mark for bringing everyone together. Then he paused. He had more to say.

"This is our last Christmas," he began. He tried to go on, but his face crumpled, his tears began to flow. "Damn it to hell." And digging into his pocket, he pulled out his handkerchief and cursed himself for being an old fool.

My mother was sitting on a cushion on the chair beside him, looking down, that tender smile of hers playing across her face. Stu's gaze was fixed on his plate, discomfort perhaps. Others were sending encouraging looks Dad's way. Al was. Ben was. I think they were, anyway. My eyes were so full of tears I could barely see.

Finally, he collected himself and began again. "She always insisted that you be treated the same," he said. "She was a wonderful mother. She insisted there be no prejudice. Nothing special for the boys that the girls wouldn't also have, and nothing for the girls that the boys also wouldn't have. That was the *only* thing she insisted on. The rest she let be. And we've had a wonderful life together."

He sat down, mortified by his loss of control. I wasn't the only one who felt proud of him and moved. He had found the right generous words, even if they weren't everything he had intended to say, even if in his summing-up there was oversimplification and whitewashing, and even if I didn't see how he could possibly know they would be dead by next Christmas. People lived on and on in the retirement home, on and on and on.

Later, I asked Al, "What did Dad *mean* when he said this was their last Christmas?"

My brother eyed me sardonically before saying, "He meant exactly what he said."

This was typical. What I wanted to mull over were the things my father and brother considered self-evident. Or simply didn't care to analyze. I wanted to know what Dad sensed in himself that made him so certain. Was he guessing or did he know, and if he knew, how did he know? More often than not, his dire blanket statements proved untrue. In the coming months we would talk about Sidney Crosby. I had taken to reading the sports pages in the newspaper so that we would have something to talk about together, and as a result

I had formed quite a bond with Sidney, especially after the two atrocious concussions that knocked him out of play. I made some mention of "my boy, who is still in a fog."

"He'll never play hockey again," my father said.

"Is that what they're saying?" Alarmed.

"He'll *never play again*."

His penchant for the emphatic negative, for ending a conversation before it began, including any future for poor Sidney.

So I did not take him literally when he said this was their last Christmas. However, that was how it turned out. Not for my mother, but for him.

HIS BOOK

ON ONE OF MY VISITS to London when my parents were in their seventies, I spent part of a morning in the small ground-floor room that was my mother's first studio. In Wiarton she had painted in the back kitchen where Jet slept in an old easy chair. In Mitchell she used Dad's study while he was at work, or the kitchen table. In Guelph—where? In the basement, perhaps, or was it in the garage? Only in 1969, when they built their house in London, did she finally have this tiny studio of her own, and only in 1984, when she was sixty-five, did she have the big studio built onto the northwest side of the house.

Around me the walls were spattered with paint, although everything was neat, all the surfaces clean. Yew bushes darkened the lower half of the window. I was alone in the house, my parents having gone for a walk with Uncle Al, who had driven up from Maine, where he had moved after he retired. I was writing in my notebook, seated at the grey Arborite table that would later travel to the retirement home in Ottawa.

I found myself picturing my father at his desk on the other side of the wall, sending his long scrawl across page after page, and the parallel jolted me. The ultimate similarity. We were both aspiring writers. What he had planned as a research paper on former students had turned into a memoir.

———

That morning at breakfast Uncle Al had talked about how much he'd loved *Tom Sawyer* as a boy, more than any other book, and how hard he had laughed when he first read it. He quoted the opening lines with gusto: "'"Tom!" No answer.'" Delighting as much in the recollection of his own amusement as in the book itself.

For a long time I had wanted this articulate, thoughtful, fluent letter-writer of an uncle to adopt me. In rather idolizing him when I was a teenager and young woman, I was taking my cue from my father. "I had an older brother who was very good to me," he said once, explaining how as a boy he had an archery set that was the envy of the neighbourhood—it was a gift from his brother, older by eight years. The only serious argument the two of them ever had, as far as I know, was about private education versus public. My uncle had devoted his career to the first and my father to the second. I wasn't around for the argument. It came at the tail end of their trip together on the Trans-Siberian Railway, a journey during which my father must have fallen into his old role of adoring younger brother, at least until his temper flared.

My uncle said he still laughed aloud when he was reading alone in his house. He would crack up and positively roar with laughter.

My father turned to me. "That's how we're different. He was always that way and I never was. I could never see it. A hockey game—I enjoyed it, but I never got carried away. I never *expressed* myself. He's never had any trouble expressing himself."

The concept behind his memoir was a good one. He would track down the five students from whom he had expected the most and the five from whom he had expected the least and find out what had become of them. In the process he would recreate the times and life of a teacher and high school principal in small-town Ontario in the 1950s and '60s.

We were at the lake when he gave me a copy of the finished book. It was raining, I remember, and in the afternoon, while it continued to rain and the others went fishing, he perused what I had lent him, *The First Man* by Camus, and I read his book. He had not been able to find a publisher in the end, so had chosen the printing firm that gave him the lowest bid and published it himself. As I turned the pages, sloppy errors in typesetting made me wince and then a paragraph made me freeze. He had been criticized, he wrote, for strapping two senior boys for throwing chalk. What amazed me was that he admitted it, and admitted it so freely, agreeing in hindsight with the school trustees who thought he should have found another way, though they upheld him. "I am sure they were probably right," he wrote. A classic half-admission, neither grudging nor wholehearted. Only "probably right."

His image of himself as a young teacher was so different from my impression of him. "Self-confident, ambitious and undoubtedly brash," he wrote. Did he lose the self-confidence later, or never have it to the degree he thought, or have it more than I realized? Or did he have it out in the world and not at home, or with others and not with me? Barely a day went by when he didn't castigate himself for some stupidity. But what's to stop a person from feeling stupid and intelligent at the same time? Nothing.

I made a pot of tea and took my father a cup filled to the brim, scalding black the way he liked it. We drank our tea together in the cabin and I told him I was enjoying his book. Then in a cowardly if understandable act of avoidance I steered the conversation toward the thing that every writer hates most: discussion of a different, better book. I had felt close to my father the whole time I read *The First Man*, Camus's unfinished tale of his youth, found in the wreckage of the fatal car crash and published posthumously many years later. Camus was his sort of boy: tough, tanned, covered in dust, fearless, devoted to his mother. I saw my father as a boy whacking his tennis ball off the garage doors, whacking his lacrosse ball off the cement foundation under the kitchen window and Gracie never minding. Her last child, her rough and rugged companion with the big grin.

I had hesitated before lending him the book, suspecting he might think I was criticizing him instead of offering him a compliment. In fact, I was trying to do both, trying to get closer to him while not giving an inch. I knew the book was likely to make him feel both inadequate and consoled: like Camus as a boy and unlike Camus as a man. Like Camus's beloved teacher, who had also used corporal punishment and refused to apologize, and unlike him, for Camus's teacher had never lost control of himself, never run amok, never got nicknamed "Gordon the warden."

I asked him what he thought of the book so far, and he had to look away. It had moved him, as I knew it would. But mixed into his reaction was disappointment that I wasn't more enthusiastic about what he had written. I did not tell him his book was terrific, because it wasn't. I told him it was interesting and honest.

On the last day at the cabin, five-year-old Sochi sat beside him on his bunk and went through his wallet with great interest. Then she took my mother's hairbrush (the handle broken off long ago), stood up and brushed what little hair he had left. He sat like a lamb. It occurred to me, watching them, that he was disarmed by her complete lack of fear. And what a gift that was to him.

How differently they worked, my father and mother. In doing the research for his book my father had used a questionnaire, never deviating from the set questions no matter how interesting the answer, never revisiting the student to get more information. It was a shy, formal, textbook approach, his material defined by his inability or unwillingness to pursue it further. My mother, though not without doubts and inhibitions, opened herself up to her subject and to her materials with an appetite that was infectious. She had what my father admired more than anything else: she had personality. And she had what I most admired: passionate creative energy.

During a Christmas visit, my father made an arresting remark about himself. "My father didn't think much of me," he said, staring down at his placemat, fingering his serviette. "The sun rose and set on my brother." He gave a shrug, "But that was all right. I didn't think much of him either."

He could have taken the words right out of my mouth.

I said as much to my mother the next time we were alone together. I speculated that having a father who doesn't think much of you surely explained his self-contempt, at least in part.

"I'm not sure," she said. "He really didn't think much of his father. And his mother adored him. He had the most secure of childhoods, I don't know why he doesn't have a higher opinion of himself. It's a mystery."

The look on her face remained unconvinced when I said I understood his contempt and his anger. "You always say he doesn't really mean it. He does mean it. You hate conflict,"

I went on. "You don't feel contempt for people. *He* does. *I* do. We're the same in this. And we hate ourselves for it."

Her eyes went on hold while I said this. She did not want to believe any of it, not even that I understood him or that we were alike.

How hard it must have been for her to be caught between us, to hear me say I didn't think much of the man she had married.

"He was disappointed in your reaction to his book," she told me. "But he also said, 'Well, what else could she say?'"

For the record, never once did my father offer a reaction to any of my books.

His sits in front of me now. *Those Were the Days: The Ontario Secondary School, 1945-1970.* It's summertime. Again I'm at the lake. I have been putting off the job of rereading its 145 pages. The weight of my feelings about him makes it almost impossible to start.

But I start. The first pages have straightforward strength and some humility. "There is no intention to suggest that the quarter century of *Those Were the Days* is any better or any worse than any other twenty-five-year period. Quite simply, they are the years which are familiar to me and the years which were also good to me."

My father.

Soon, though, I find myself supplying missing commas, questioning his generalizations about the world, wishing he had more subtlety and depth. The sociology-speak of his questions irks me, as does his phrase "life success" and his ranking of students into poor, good, above average, superior; also his clear preference for people with important and recognizable careers.

Then he swings me back onto his side. "With no sense of inadequacy but with a lot of hard work, I assumed responsibility for teaching history to every grade in the school." Certain grace notes, like that one, give a fuller flavour of him, a fuller sweep to his thoughts.

Sun appears through cloud. I take a half-full basket of strawberries down to the little dock, dunk the basket and watch the berries float up but not away. Hermit thrushes sing deep in the woods. A deer across the bay retreats from the water's edge, moves like a shadow behind trees.

I remember him opening the front door to Eden, a high school friend, wild in dress and manner, at least for our corner of Ontario. She would tell me later how welcoming he had been, what an unforgettable smile he had. Most adults, she said, reacted to her with alarm. "Your father impressed me," she said.

My friend Sheila never ceased to enjoy the way he poked fun at us and at himself. She called him the old philosopher, which flattered and delighted him. Through her eyes, I saw him as she did, self-deprecating, kindly, refusing to take anyone too seriously. I remember her laughing at something he said, leaning over to her husband and remarking fondly, "I can just hear my father saying that."

My parents called each other "love" when I was a child. Often he ran his hand up the inside of my mother's dress and always she responded with low-throated sounds, like someone falling into bed after hours of hard labour. He had good eyes and good teeth and beautiful hands as well as those fine legs. He walked with a confident stride, with conviction.

They were twenty-three when they married. The day I picked those beautiful tulips as a small child, in all innocence it seems to me, they would have been in their early thirties and worried about what the Cheethams would think, Mr. Cheetham being a dentist and moneyed, and my father only a high school teacher. I have a vague memory of Mrs. Cheetham telephoning my mother to complain. Out of social worry, they punished me, when all they had to do was ask me not to pick other people's flowers. All they had to do was talk to me.

Yet my first memory is of something my father said to me alone. I was about two years old, lying flat on my back on the grassy slope beside our house in Owen Sound, staring up at creamy-white clouds rolling in with their look of endless summer, and revelling in the picnic promised for later in the day. His feet walked past my head and his voice, always ready for regret, said, "I hope those clouds don't mean rain."

My father cared enough about his students to wonder what had become of them, to seek them out and interview them, to take pains to write about them generously yet honestly. I like what he's done. I find it engrossing, more so this time through, which is my third, for in fact I reread the book some years ago after my mother said he was disappointed by my reaction. I made a point of telling him I was rereading his book and enjoying it very much. *You* write well, I told him later as we talked at the dining room table, stressing it, overstressing it, perhaps.

And what am I doing now but what my mother did her whole married life? Wishing I could make him feel better about himself.

Wishing—and this is me, not my mother—I could be fairer to him.

In 1947, when he started at his first school, "bread was 12 cents a loaf (a cent extra for sliced bread), milk was 10 cents a quart, and doctors made house calls for $3.00." Those first three years of teaching were his happiest. "Never again would I experience, to the same degree, the thrill of self-discovery. I had learned that I could arouse the interest and enthusiasm of students, whether in the classroom or on the playing field." As a going-away gift his home class presented him with prints of *The West Wind* by Tom Thomson and *North Shore, Lake Superior* by Lawren Harris, which he hung in the school office as long as he was a principal. In his book he revisits his time at the five high schools at which he toiled, then does longer profiles of the students he selected. On every page I get the impression of a diffident man, truly curious about others and eager to give them their due without abandoning his signature bluntness. For instance, a boy who came from a very poor family and whose work life my father describes as "anything but one-dimensional" remembered my father returning his history examination paper with the comment, "It is the best thing you have done, I could understand what you were saying."

My father, who played football, hockey and lacrosse in university and received the Athletic Stick in 1940, takes special pains with the student he least understands, a bachelor and church organist. Piano-playing boys were never his forte. It touches me, his deliberate appreciation of someone with a story to tell "that sets him apart from his classmates." Just as I'm touched when he says of someone who went on to work as an editor for a major book publisher that he hopes she will attempt some original writing. "I suspect there is a talent that has yet to be revealed."

Now I have to wonder if he came to my books as I came to his, expecting to be embarrassed. At the end of his life, when he packed up his study before the move to Ottawa, he winnowed his library, selecting the books that mattered to him, leaving the rest behind for his children to dispose of. Among the ones left behind were all of mine. I stepped into his dismantled study and saw all seven of them, abandoned on a lower shelf.

I leaned down and picked up a few of these rejects, read the inscriptions I had written to him and my mother in each book, then sank to the floor and sat there for a while. Wasn't there even one he valued enough to keep on his shelves?

Had his father loved him as much as he loved his first son, would my father have been as confident as his brother? Uncle Al's letters seemed effortless. He had a flare for humour and an enviable grasp of American politics and the state of the world. A letter from Uncle Al was an event.

We all expected a book from Uncle Al, but it never came. He wrote a short, good, valuable memoir about the Hays, for family consumption, and an entertaining report of a trip to England he made with his father in the 1950s. That's all that I'm aware of. My father wrote his shorter, less personal, less satisfying family history, again for family consumption. He also wrote a history of the John Howard Society of Ontario, the prison-reform organization he volunteered with for thirty-seven years. It's a spiral-bound report, forty-four pages long, that I have never even leafed through. Not until this morning, when I opened it rather idly and started to read. First one astonishing thing happened and then another.

In describing a man born in 1726, my father could be describing himself. "John Howard must have been a strange and complex individual who could not have been everyone's cup of tea. Having been left a comfortable fortune and all the family's property he was generous and caring to the tenants on his estate at Cardington in the county of Bedford, England. Still, he was a difficult and lonely man who, despite a great reputation, was to some extent a personal failure. He failed as a parent to his only son and he lacked those qualities which would have enabled him to establish close personal relations of friendship." It's one of those instances where the writer seems privy to true understanding and no small sympathy.

My father goes on to say that John Howard's achievement "derives not so much from personal courage and prison visitation, important as these were. Rather, his reputation rests on the meticulous recording and reporting of what he saw, in order that the general public might be made aware. His book, *The State of Prisons in England and Wales*, had three editions in his lifetime."

His own report, I am sorry to say, soon becomes larded with research about criminal legislation, constitutional change, levels of government, organizational minutiae. I start to skip, then pause over the name of one of the men he cites—Joseph McCulley, Deputy Commissioner of Penitentiaries—wondering if it could be the same man, the famous headmaster of Pickering, the private school my father attended in his last two years of high school. Some quick research tells me that it is. A bit more produces a newspaper article from 1929 about McCulley's storied opposition to corporal punishment. "We do not think punishment has any good effect on a boy and we don't think that it is necessary. Punishment begets a sort of resentment which will never go away."

I lean back in my chair, my head ablaze. *This* is what my father came from, this bed of roses, this progressive school where mutual respect between teacher and student flowed from the Quaker belief that any use of physical force was wrong. "There is an atmosphere of home about it, and the boys are not afraid of us."

No wonder my father didn't have a higher opinion of himself. Every time he used the strap or the back of his hand, he was deviating from principles he knew very well. More had been expected of him, and he had expected more of himself. After all, in that special school where moral, cultural and intellectual vigour were prized, he had shone like his brother before him. Each in turn had received the Garrett Cane award bestowed by student vote on the one who would best represent the ideals and life of the school.

A tall order for a man as difficult and essentially lonely as my father.

I remember lifting down from the wall of his study the photograph of him taken at Pickering. I did this when he was very old. The photograph showed the student council with my father in the middle of the front row—he was head boy—the headmaster behind him, and the rest of the students on either side. I brought it upstairs and asked him to identify who was who. Extending the middle finger of his left hand, he pointed to the boy on the far left and said he was good fun, he didn't care one bit about schoolwork, he was killed in the war; the boy at the other end was a good football player who went to McGill and became a lawyer; the two at the back were always having fun, they put peanut butter on the toilet seats; another boy was the son of the man who owned the newspaper in Lethbridge. He went on, speaking with fond and clear recollections about these people in his past, while my eyes kept returning to him—my father—in the photograph. Of all the boys, he was the one who looked far and away the most confident and at ease. He held himself so well. And that million-dollar smile of his knocked you flat.

I said admiringly how well he looked in his suit and vest, his necktie, dark socks, dark shoes; how impressively put together. "That's Granny," he said immediately. Gracie had purchased his clothes and taught him how to wear them.

But it was him too: his handsomeness, his physical ease. He was a boy a mother would be proud of, a boy a mother had doted on, a boy from a good home. All of these descriptions came to mind as I examined the photograph I knew well enough, but was only now appreciating.

On his shelves, mixed in with other books, was the small library he had received for winning the history prize in 1938 for his essay about the secret of heroism. Each book, from *War and Peace* to *The Outline of Man's Work and Wealth*, had glued inside the front cover a large nameplate inscribed with his name and the motto: If I Lose Myself, I Save Myself. They were words that struck deep the first time I read them. I would have been twelve or thirteen and intent on examining his books. The quotation—Tennyson's—ignited a feeling and urged a direction that I understood instinctively and hungered after. My father might well have felt the same.

Also on his shelves was his faded-red copy of *Huck Finn* signed and inscribed by his teacher, Florence McIlraith. *To Gordon Hay for achieving the highest grades in his examinations leaving Junior III and entering Senior III. 1930.* Yet he was forever convinced that his brother was the smart one. Or to be more precise, the smarter. He wasn't wrong. But it's too bad he couldn't take more pleasure in being smart enough. In the last year of his life, not once but twice he brought up his brother's response to the thesis he had written for his master's degree, a treatise on preparing teenagers for citizenship by teaching them history. "My brother thought it was *bunk*," he said. I said I didn't think that could be true. He made a face and shrugged. It was absolutely true. Irrefutable. And it stung him still.

Assessing his various hurts as I walk beside the canal one day, a memory surfaces of his reaction to learning I had drawn his name for the Christmas gift-giving: "That means a book," with a dismissive downturn of his mouth.

> *Gordon the warden, you do me wrong*
> *To think I don't know your love of song*
> *Or the foods you crave*
> *And how you would behave*
> *If you could. (And you should.)*

The canal's still waters curve beside me, brimming with summer, and I find myself giving him the gifts I never gave him. Even the requisite poem comes easily. In our family a gift had to be accompanied by a poem. *Gordon the warden*, I say again, *you do me wrong*. And from under the tree I pull out a box and place it at his feet. He has to bend down to open it and then unwrap, one at a time, the series of gifts inside: a jar of lemon curd, a russet apple, a box set of Gilbert and Sullivan, a new chamois for polishing windows and the car, a recording by Sir Thomas Beecham of "Jerusalem."

In actuality, I did give him a book, probably the biography of his hero Paul Robeson, which generated a letter that was like a dry book report and made me wonder why he couldn't communicate with me like a normal human being. But in my mind I am doing what I wish I had done. *Open this box and feel ashamed / Not-a-book, you old fool / not-a-book after another / instead, what proves you're as well loved as your brother.* An excellent atlas, an Eccles cake, new pegs for his cribbage board, finger-less gloves for his indoor hands, llama-wool socks for his chilly feet. Best of all, a visit to Question Period on Parliament Hill that I could have arranged and he would have enjoyed, the old history teacher staring down at what he used to teach. He has to pause in the unwrapping, so pleased and mollified is he that he can't help but start to laugh with near-boyish pleasure.

It's almost as good as if it had really happened. For an hour beside the canal, I have the satisfaction of beating him into submission with my gifts, inducing the sheepish acknowledge-ment that he has underestimated me. I know you, my gifts say.

HIS END

IN THE MONTHS BEFORE he died I used to rub lotion into the top of his head, the bald pate crusted with scurf that he picked at constantly. He bent his head while I worked in the lotion and said thank you afterwards. He was in chronic pain. It felt like he was sitting on a sword, he said. Pain kept shooting up his back. We went to specialists, but when they suggested any sort of procedure my father refused. He really did have a memorable NO. Sweeping, magisterial. No to everything the urologist recommended. He wasn't looking to enter a marathon of exploratory tests. "Maybe ten or twenty years ago my answer would have been different." He would have liked relief from the pain, but not enough to undergo treatment or take medication. "No, damn no, to any more damn pills!"

I continued to telephone him every morning around nine in order to orient him for the day. If I failed to make the call, or was late, my phone would ring and his voice would blast, "What the *hell* is going on?"

I remember the February morning when great gusts of snow were swirling past my windows and I was fifteen minutes late. "I'm late to school!" I laughed nervously when he picked up the phone, and so it felt, the twelve-year-old in hot water. That morning we talked about snow days past, how the telephone would ring off the hook in Mitchell with parents wanting to know if the buses were cancelled. Our memories transported me back to his school on the outskirts of town—that scene of being led down the hall on a Saturday morning and put in an empty classroom to study for approaching exams. The fluorescent lights, the blackboards that were green, the echoing quiet of a room filled with desks in rows, myself undefended and surrounded by what was looming—exams, yes, but also my father in his office down the hall.

In those last months of his life, we got along better than we ever had. In fairness and accuracy, despite what I've written, I should say that we got along more often than not during the whole of their time in Ottawa. We sparred regularly, but we were closer to each other too, partly because conversation with my mother was often impossible and partly because I let up and extended myself toward him.

I admitted as much to a friend when we drove one summer afternoon to a lake in the Gatineau Hills. In the parking lot, next to a grove of white pines, the act of slamming the trunk shut flooded me with my father's filthy mood before any trip, and I said how much hatred I had felt for him over the years. "But we get along now," I said. "All I had to do was kiss him. Give him affection. The affection I never gave him and that he was so hungry for."

That made my friend lean against the car and say tearfully, "Oh, Lizzie."

Early on in their time in Ottawa, I had seen the effect on my father of receiving a kiss from me. He softened visibly, melted a bit every time. So I made a conscious decision to always kiss him as soon as I arrived for a visit and again before I left.

In those last months we even bantered on the telephone. "It's Laurence Olivier," he said one morning, and I laughed and asked him how he was. "Laurence Olivier is always good."

"Then I must be Vivien Leigh."

I reminded him that the shuffleboard tournament was later in the day and he said it wasn't. "That's on Tuesday," he said, "today is Monday." I told him today was Tuesday. "It's got a nerve," he said.

That spring he became an old man hawking up phlegm. Finally he was using a cane—his prize cane, naturally, the Garrett cane; he refused any other—and he even agreed to try a walker, though once it arrived it sat in a corner untouched. When I told the doctor that my father had yielded enough to have a walker but not enough to use it, he laughed and said he had a patient who didn't like pills; she was housebound, so he would visit her at home and ask her if she had been taking her pills. "No," she would say, "but I sleep with them under the pillow."

That summer Dad was more and more unsteady on his feet. At times he had real trouble moving his legs. In July he announced that he wasn't writing any more letters. When the following day a letter arrived from Jeannie, Mom read it and said she should answer it; she would. Dad barked out, "You won't. No more letters!"

His scalp got even more crusted and scurfy. The space on his head that I was willing to kiss narrowed drastically. The area around his ear was safe.

"Your mother is such a pissmire," he said one day.

And she in return, "He asks damn double-barrelled, irresistible, devastating questions."

His question, apparently, was why neither of them liked to join in the chatty social events in the residence. Dad had wanted her to explain why. Another day he said to her, "Are you reading the book about the Rubicon? Do you know what you're reading? What's it about?"

"The investigation of . . ." She petered out.

"Who crossed the Rubicon?" he demanded.

"Caesar, for one."

"He was the *only* one."

"Well, that's not how I understood it."

"And why did he cross the Rubicon? Who was his big rival?"

"The name doesn't come."

And on it went.

One day he said to me, "Do you know what happened this morning? Your mother didn't know how to get dressed. She didn't know which came first, her shoes or her pants."

"That's true," Mom said. "Stupid." And turning to Dad: "It was stupid, if you want to know."

"And I didn't know either," Dad said flatly, in his first-ever admission that their minds were on a par.

In August, thinking there might be some obvious source of trouble we were overlooking, I asked the doctor to examine all of him. He had Dad stretch out on his bed. He examined his rectum, his prostate, his heart, and pronounced him in good shape. Later, alone in the hallway with the doctor, I reported my father's gloomy view that he wasn't going to see Jeannie again, "Because I'll be dead." The doctor thought that was just depression talking. There was no reason in his view that my sister needed to speed up the visit she had planned for September.

It being August, we had peaches in a basket on the kitchen counter, tomatoes in another basket, and soon there would be blueberries.

We brought my parents home for a lunch of fresh corn, buttered toast, fresh tomato. At our kitchen table my mother buttered her cob copiously before she ate it slowly, thoroughly, going around it a second time after the kernels were gone, buttering it again, then sucking out the juices. "Thank you totally," she said when she was done. "In the eclipsean way of speaking, all thanks to you."

In Renfrew her family had grown their own corn in their big garden. The rule was that you got the water boiling on the stove, then dashed out to pick the corn, and once you had your arms full, you raced back. If you tripped on the way, it was too late, the corn wouldn't be fresh. She claimed that once she had eaten thirteen cobs in a single sitting. "Well, some of them were small," she allowed.

Back at the residence, she showed me her treasures, things she had pocketed on their walks. They were products, my father said dryly, of the Stevenson Crouch; an old joke of his and a good one that went back to the days before they were married when my mother trained her eyes on the sidewalk, so he claimed, in order to spot any loose change on the ground. The treasures were arranged on a green-and-red Christmas napkin: two dark feathers, a sticker from a piece of fruit, a silver top from a juice bottle, and a bit of shingle etched with lichen. She wasn't sure what she would do with them, she said, but she thought they were beautiful. And they were, laid out like that.

Yet another version of Al's portrait was in the works. My brother had scanned the original photograph from 1952 and sent her enlargements so that she had the image to work with again. Mark, standing beside her, asked, "Did he catch anything?"

"No," she laughed. "But he was *hounding* them."

This time she was using pastels and pencil, staying small-scale and simple. It would turn out to be a reasonable portrait by a reasonable person, a clear sketch of a small boy holding his fishing pole, the last piece of art she ever made.

By September there wasn't much Gordon left on Gordon Hay's bones. He wasn't eating anymore, except for occasional pieces of orange and banana, the odd digestive cookie, the liquid food substitute Ensure, and tea. He spent much of his time in bed. One day, after taking Mom down to the dining room, I went back to their rooms to gather up on a tray all the dishes of uneaten food that had accumulated in their small fridge, and I caught sight of him on his way to the bathroom. He was wearing the unbuttoned blue shirt I had put on him when he sat up for tea, his hands were down at his crotch, holding his underwear in place, and his legs were pencils. The shrivelled shanks of myth, of old kings. In that moment I understood as I never had before the meaning of "on his last legs."

The doctor came by while Dad was still in the bathroom. "How is he?" he asked. There was an alertness on his part, as if something dramatic were in the wind.

"I don't know," I said. "You'll tell me if I need to call my siblings?"

"Sometimes it's hard to tell," he said. But yes, he would tell me.

The next day I went over in the morning and he was doing better. He sat up in bed and had a cup of tea. He was very gentle with Mom, holding her hand, stroking her arm.

I took her into the courtyard, to a bench in the sun, and asked her what she was thinking about. She said she was trying to get used to the idea of being dead. "Things quieten down," she said. "If he goes, he's had a wonderful life and you've been part of it." A pause. "But what are you going to do when we die?"

"Do you mean how are we going to manage without you?"

"No, no. What are you going to do with the bones?"

We would do as she and Dad wanted: cremation and the ashes spread at the cabin. I asked if she was worried about dying. She said no, but she wished they could have one of those ten-minute pills.

Later that day Dad lost control of his bowels while he lay in bed and there was a lot to clean up. Afterwards, when he was back sitting on the side of his bed, he fiddled with his facecloth, folding and refolding it, then placed it beside his pillow and lay down. He told me I would need to arrange with someone downstairs to bring Mom back up to the rooms when she finished her dinner. "Last night she got lost."

"I did," she agreed.

I made arrangements with the staff to shepherd her back and forth. That weekend, Labour Day weekend, Mark and I went to the cabin for two days, and when we got back to town, in the late afternoon, we went directly to the residence rather than first going home. Dad was in bed and shocking to see. Something drastic had happened. His face was darker and hollowed out, and he seemed smaller, weaker, a dying man. With much effort and obvious pain, he rose to sit, swinging his legs over the side of the bed, resting his feet on the floor. I sat near him at the foot of his bed. I asked him if he wanted me to call Al, Jeannie and Stu and tell them to come.

"I'm not hollering that this is my last," he said.

He drank the tea I made. When Mark took my mother down for dinner, I peeled an orange and half a banana, which he ate: all of the banana, most of the orange. He refused the Ensure.

His feet and knees were a splotchy purple. I sat on the floor and rubbed his feet. I suggested I trim his toenails. "Not now," he said. I sat beside him again on the edge of the bed. He bent over and ran his finger between each of his toes to remove lint, a methodical act I had seen him perform since the beginning of time. Then, with another huge expenditure of effort, he raised one leg onto the bed. I helped lift the other. He lowered himself with difficulty onto the pillow. I tucked another pillow in behind to raise his head.

Sitting again on the edge of his bed, I asked, "What are you thinking, Dad?"

Long pause. Then, "Okay." It was one of the words he used to say a conversation was over.

I told him that tomorrow was the first day of school, that Ben had called from Montreal, amazed that for the first September in eighteen years he would be doing something other than attending his first class.

"And he has his whole lifetime ahead of him," my father said, shaking his head in what seemed like despairing wonder.

It turned out he had fallen in the bathroom the night before and had had a hard time of it, according to the nurse who filled in Mark and my mother when they went down to the dining room. That's why he had deteriorated so rapidly. My mother had slept through the night, so hadn't been aware. When they rejoined us, Mark asked him about the fall, and Dad said, "I did something I shouldn't have done." He wouldn't say more.

Mom's eyes were on his bruised knees. "Those are emphatic emphases on your knees," she said.

At home I telephoned Al, who said he would come the next day. I called Stu and Jeannie. They would wait to see how things unfolded.

Early the next morning I went over. At one moment, while Dad slept, Mom said, "I've never been this close to death in process before."

We sat with him while he slept on. One of the nurses told me later that she had found my mother in bed with him and had discouraged her; it was unsafe, she said. I was sorry she took that view. I told her it was fine; they needed to be together. It's true the bed was a twin bed and hardly spacious, but my mother was small.

The doctor came by later and asked my father how he felt.

"*Rotten*." As only he could say it, putting the full weight of his limitless disgust into the word.

"If you want to feel better," the doctor said to him, "drink fluids. If you want to feel worse, don't. And I know you're an intelligent enough man to know what I'm saying."

"I want to feel better," my father said.

I assumed he meant he wanted to get better, but that isn't, in fact, what he said. I don't know when I began to understand that the previous December's declaration about this being their last Christmas had been not a premonition but a decision. Even at this stage it wasn't clear to me—perhaps it wasn't clear to him—since he continued to eat a little and to drink.

I had to go downtown that week to do an interview and afterwards I dropped into the National Gallery, where on the second floor I came to the painting of an old and depleted man by Jan Lievens, Dutch, 1607–74. It was Job in a grey loincloth, otherwise naked, sitting on his dung heap. Thin arms, sunken chest, white beard, bare purply feet. I realized that whenever I wanted to see my dying father again, all I had to do was come to the Gallery and sit in front of this painting.

Al arrived. We went over and Dad was flushed, his hands fussing around his neck, one finger tracing something in the air above his chest. Al went to the side of his bed and Dad caught sight of him. This too was biblical. He reached out and clasped my brother's forearm, above the wrist, happier to see him than he knew how to express. I thought of Jacob seeing Joseph again, and when I got home I looked it up in Genesis. "Now let me die since I have seen your face and you are still alive."

Over the next few days, Dad lay on his back, sleeping most of the time, mouth open. He didn't feel better. It hurt him to swallow water or juice. The act of swallowing set up a cough, like a painful dry heave. We got ice and crushed it in a towel with a hammer; he liked the pieces of ice on his tongue. When we told him a hospital bed would be arriving later in the day, he said, "When will the stairway to heaven be here?" Then he answered himself, "Tomorrow."

Certain nurses were particularly fond of him. "She cares," he said of one. As with the charmer from Newfoundland, the first director of care, he was like a lamb with these women, smiling, responding, boylike. They must have seen in him a man who for more than two years had taken exceptional care of his wife, a gruff old man in pain, a patriarch coming to the end of his life. The receptionist at the front desk, who had always taken a special and affectionate interest in my parents, teasing my father and enlisting him in the beanbag-throwing competitions and any other activities she could dream up, came to their rooms to see him. She stood beside his bed and took his hand. My father smiled and relaxed. "Tell me a story," Dee asked.

"Only one story," he said. "I'm glad you came into my life."

He had the gift, my father, of saying exactly the right thing when he chose to. I remember how some months into their first year in the retirement home, my mother had fretted about burdening me. We were having our regular Sunday dinner in my kitchen and she said, "You're doing too much. We shouldn't come every Sunday. We take up too much of your time. It's too much."

Dad said, "It's what I look forward to all week."

She was adamant. "We shouldn't impose every week. Every other week is plenty."

I thought how much easier that would be, every other week. I said, "But we like having you here. We like your company."

My mother shook her head. No one said anything for a moment. She turned to Dad. "You're not saying anything."

He gazed at her. "I think you're very lucky. We're both very lucky to have them here. And no one deserves it more than you."

Later in the day, I went back to spell off Al, and Dad said to us, "What's burning?"

"Nothing is burning, Dad."

"Over there." He pointed to the left. "And in that corner over there." He pointed to the right.

I put some tiny pieces of fresh peach on his tongue. He pointed across the room. "What's that?"

"What?" We tried to see what he was pointing at.

"A helmet," he said. "Full of ropes. A sweater. And over there." Then he added, as if to himself, "They're not to be trusted."

I brought from the chest of drawers the photograph of Gracie in her wedding dress, thinking the sight of his mother might be of comfort. (I don't know how religious he was at this stage. I think he still believed in God. It was possible he thought there was an afterlife, but it was nothing he ever talked about. He had severed his connection with the Quakers when he and my mother moved to Ottawa, just as he had ended their practice of donating to numerous charities.) He took the photograph from my hands and studied it, then, pointing his finger at Gracie, he brought out the unshakable opinion he had stuck to all his life: "She should have married Uncle Hugh."

Will I go to my grave thinking my mother should have married another man? Someone more attuned to the creative life, who could have cooked for himself and put in his own eye drops? Who didn't fly off the handle at the drop of a hat? Not anymore. Not after seeing how woven into each other, body and soul, the two of them were.

He closed his eyes, and I asked, "When do you want Jeannie to come?"

"Today," he said.

"Stu, too," I said.

He nodded.

Over the next couple of days everyone arrived, Stu and his wife, my sister, Sochi and Ben. They would stay, on and off, until the end. Sochi and Jeannie went over together in the evening and found Al stretched out on Mom's bed reading *Life of Pi*, while Mom sat on a chair between the two beds holding Dad's hand. The night before, when I'd dropped by, Al was lying on his stomach beside her and reading *Potluck Pogo* aloud, the two of them convulsed with helpless laughter. It's a scene I often think about: my brother stretched diagonally across her bed, my mother with her knees tucked up to make room, like a girl being read to, and Dad resting in the bed beside them. My brother knew what was needed and provided it, as June rain satisfies the eager ground.

I recalled then that on Al's birthday, which was June 8th, and this would have been their first June in Ottawa, I was walking with Mom and Dad in the residence courtyard and she was remembering how Al emerged from the womb sucking his thumb—so unusual, she said, that he would be sucking his thumb when they brought him back to her after washing him—and how vigorous he was, kicking his feet, eager to stand. Such a contrast to the scrawny, premature mite Stu had been. In July they took him to Hurds Lake ("The place I love to hate," interjected Dad; my mother's childhood lake near Renfrew and populated with too many Stevensons for my father's taste) and it was the last time they were there, she said. In August Dad picked tobacco for extra money before his teaching job began in September; he did that for the two summers they lived in Tillsonburg. "In those days our energy was *appalling*," my mother said.

Now it was surely the last September of my father's life. My mother said to Sochi, "He's not long for this land. I've never watched someone die before. I'm going to stay right here. I'm sorry if it interrupts your visit."

And to Jeannie she said, "Maybe you can clarify this for me. Am I north or south of the border?"

"You're north of the border," Jeannie said. "You're in Canada."

"And all these paintings on the wall. I know they're mine. But did they bring them here?"

"They did."

"That's amazing," Mom said.

Dad asked for his glasses the next time I was there. He said he couldn't see. When he put them on and looked at me, it was without recognition. His eyes had dimmed, filmed over. As a snake's eyes turn bluish, so I've read, before shedding its skin. His fingers fussed at his throat. After I put salve on his swollen lips, he smoothed them with his fingertips, then reached into his mouth and probed everywhere with his fingers.

"Dad, what are you doing?"

"I don't know."

He probed around his mouth, reaching in and pulling out his tongue.

"Dad," Al said, taking his hands and putting them on his chest. "You're going to hurt yourself."

Outside, the September weather was all you could wish for, days of sunshine and light buoyant air followed by clear nights with a waxing moon. One afternoon I read the opening pages of *Moby-Dick* to my mother (after her tea, her lemon tart, her piece of chocolate) and she listened intently. She had been immersing herself in the story once again, looking up from its pages to announce that it was a *wonderful* book and she had *never* read it before. "He takes those words by the armpits," she said admiringly.

About a dozen pages in, Dad said from his bed, "That's good, what you read."

I was surprised and pleased. I had thought him asleep and unaware.

The next day Nasrin, a nurse who cared deeply for Dad and never tired of telling me what a good father he was, had tears in her eyes when she brought a halt to his medicine. He could not swallow it anymore, even ground up in applesauce. She had me follow her into the corridor, where she said the next step, when a patient can't swallow, is to stop medications and give morphine. She was worried about my mother. Mrs. Hay should be separated, she said, not to have to watch him die. No, I said, my mother wants to be with him until the end. But, Nasrin said, she'll have those memories with her. I said she would have a lifetime of memories.

We four siblings kept our parents company around the clock in those final days. It's a marvellous thing to be as proud of your siblings as I was. I went over one morning with a thermos of coffee to relieve Stu, who had been there all night. None of us had slept much. My mother, still in bed, said it had been a weird night. "Your dad had the worst of it with this double intercontinental drift, if that's what you call it."

She got up and went over to him. "How are you, Daddy?"

He smiled at her, one of his big smiles that I hadn't seen in quite a while.

Jeannie told me that Mom had spoken to him so sweetly. "Daddy, I know you're having a hard time saying goodbye."

His face got yellower with every passing day. One night, in her nightgown, Mom went over to the commode beside his bed and sat down and said, "We've been good friends for a long time. We've been great friends." Then she climbed into her own bed. Stu, who witnessed this and related it to me, then got into his sleeping bag in the other room, only to see her head poke around the door.

"Now, look. Tell me what's going on. What's happening? Where's Gord?"

"He's in the bed beside you."

"You're joshing. That's not Gord. That's not my husband."

"Well, you've been *together* a long time."

"Then you're his son. You don't *act* like father and son."

"Mom, you go back to bed and sleep and in the morning you'll feel better."

She went back to bed. Only to reappear a few minutes later. "Now come on," she said. "You can tell me. What's going on?"

The look on her face was half-amused, half-mystified. "It's those two imps," she said.

"Where are they?" Stu asked.

"There. Those two imps." And she pointed at the chest of drawers.

He took her back to bed and she said to him, "I'm not going to sleep a wink. I'm too mixed up."

Stu laughed as he told me about it and said she was great. "She's number one," he said.

A good palliative care nurse assessed Dad, telling us that on a scale of zero to one hundred, where one hundred was health and zero was death, he was hovering between twenty and ten. She said that once the palliative care was in place—an overnight nurse, the right medication—he would be much more comfortable. He would go quickly then.

Dad's left arm took on a tortured life of its own. It kept crooking up awkwardly, like a bird's wing, while his hands worked the air. His fingers were stiff, sometimes interlaced. At times his head was arched back and his fingers fluttered at his beard. Unseeing eyes, supplicating hands. At the same time the scurf on his scalp, the lumps and growths, magically disappeared. His skin was smooth again, young-looking.

The only way we knew to give him relief from his contortions was to take his upward-thrusting arm and press it down. Stu was at his side, following his commands. "Push! Push! Two! Two! All right. Push! Atta boy." On it went, exhausting, until at 8 p.m. they gave him a second dose of morphine and after about ten minutes the arm was finally down, relaxed, his body all relaxed, his eyes closed, asleep. Jeannie and I walked home through a beautiful strong wind, dark clouds overhead, and raised a glass to morphine.

Nasrin stopped me again in the corridor a day later. Have you told your father everything you want to tell him—that you love him? that your mother will be looked after? It seemed to me these things went without saying, but I let myself be persuaded, and this was also typical, that I would surrender to what was expected. I went to the side of my father's bed and reached for his hand. I told him I loved him, I said he had been a good father. I heard the words come out of me, statements that sounded written by someone else, hollow to my ears and I imagine to his. He did not react, not a word, until I told him not to worry about Mom, we would look after her. Then his head jerked back in protest. "What about *me*?" he erupted.

I was so nonplussed I didn't know what to say.

It seemed so outrageously self-centred, yet as much in character as one of the last words he ever spoke. "Nincompoop!" he barked, addressing Jeannie across the room. She was at his desk, her back to him, reading. She stood up, shaking her head. "I came all the way from Mexico for this?" In a final resounding punchline, while we were all still together, and after he had been silent for a long time, he announced, "I'm going to live! And the rest of you are going to hell!" The volcano had spoken.

The day he died, the tree at the foot of the garden was turning yellow and orange, every leaf. I made my trek to the retirement home a little after eight. He was moaning loudly and his left arm was up by his head and contorted again, and he was sweaty. The overnight caregiver had left at seven. I laid my head on his upper arm, and under its weight his shoulder relaxed and his arm sank to his chest. I stayed in that position for ten minutes, my arm around his neck, my head weighing down his arm, feeling his heartbeat, which seemed quick and light, talking to him, "Relax your arm, that's good," while Mom lay in the adjoining bed, awake and watching. Then I went to the telephone and called a nurse and made it urgent. But not until close to nine did he get the morphine he should have received an hour earlier.

The palliative care nurse arrived at ten and showed me how to keep his heels off the bed by using a pillow; it's on the heels that lesions form, she said. She advised me to move him every two hours, to stop the ice and swab his mouth with sponge sticks instead. I had put some bits of ice on his tongue earlier and he no longer closed his mouth to suck them; they slid around his swollen tongue. The director of care arrived, new on the job but attentive and helpful, and he and the nurse were in agreement about adding an anti-anxiety medicine to the morphine to deal with Dad's agitation. My siblings and I understood him to have days rather than hours left.

I went home and found Stu packing. He had decided not to wait for Al's arrival (Al had flown back to Halifax a few days earlier and would be returning in the afternoon) before driving home to Montreal. I needed his help with the card I was writing to my French teacher; it was her birthday and I wanted the correct words for Dad's condition. Stu provided them. "*Il meurt tranquillement.*" He is dying peacefully. With the morphine, it was true. I wrote the words on a piece of paper at the kitchen table as Stu dictated them and as Dad died, it turned out, for he took his last breath at 2:20 p.m. Jeannie was with him. His breathing stopped, she said later, and she looked up from the book she was reading at his bedside. About forty-five seconds passed. He took one more breath and didn't take another. She checked the clock to make sure of the time. Mom wasn't in the room because an aide had taken her outside for a walk.

So he was already dead, I'm guessing, when Stu and Ben and I left the house together, Stu to drive home to Montreal, Ben and I to walk to the Glebe to buy a few groceries and to visit my French teacher.

Close to four o'clock, I entered the familiar building and took the elevator up to their rooms on the second floor. Jeannie and the director of care were conferring over a sheet of paper on the round table next to Dad's desk. They turned to me, and my sister gave me the news, that Dad had died an hour and a half earlier. I stood stunned for a moment, then went over to his bed, saying, "Oh, my! Oh, my!" An old-fashioned expression, but they were the words that came. His eyes were closed, his mouth open, his head tilted a bit to the left.

The sheet and a light-blue blanket covered him up to his shoulders. His skin was yellowish and marble-like. Cool when I touched his scalp, his cheek, his ear. The rest of him was still warm.

Not lemon yellow or saffron, but old piano-key yellow.

The shock of his death merged with my disappointment that I had not been with him. It happened so fast in the end, what had taken so long to happen. Jeannie joined me and rolled back the sheet to see if his toes had curled under, as legend had it. "It's not true," she said. His legs were not blue either, as she had also heard would happen.

I had already gone to Mom, who was lying on her bed, and kissed her. I took hold of her hands.

"He had a good life," she said, "on the whole."

Her "on the whole," tempering as it did her usual grateful refrain about their wonderful lives, took me aback and soothed me. Candour, especially when it comes out of the blue, clears away the empty clichés that stifle us, and enlarges the world.

Mark and Ben arrived and they too went over to his bed. I think we were all surprised by how at ease we felt with death. There was nothing formal or embarrassed in our reactions. Ben sat down on the floor, his back against the wall, and proceeded to talk about one thing and another, keeping the mood light. He was almost twenty-three and had turned into a young man who was steadily, ardently affectionate and opinionated and funny. I went back to stand beside Dad. I touched his forehead again. I remember thinking: Now don't you wake up on me, Gordon Hay.

Mark left to meet Al, who was still in ignorance, having been en route all afternoon. The rest of us waited with Dad laid out on the bed, cooling and stiffening, though not rapidly, and turning more yellow, more marble-like, even waxier.

My brother came through the door. His head pulled in, the half smile of someone in distress who knew he was on view. He went straight over to Dad, walking with that rolling gait of his, a long stride on short legs, and I remembered my mother looking out the kitchen window in Mitchell and spotting Al and Dad across the street, walking side by side. Al, who would have been fifteen or so, had lengthened his stride to match his father's, as she pointed out with amusement and no small pleasure, delighted to have this visible proof of filial love and admiration.

Al bent down and kissed Dad on the forehead. Then he too turned his attentions to Mom.

She was very lucid. She said her only regret was that she couldn't "take the same pill." Al sat beside her on the bed and put his arm around her.

I recounted how I had told Dad that we would look after her, and his "What about *me*?" His dying "*me too*."

"I already told him that," Al said to Mom. "I told him we were going to put you on eBay and auction you off to the highest bidder."

"Wrapped or unwrapped?" my mother said.

Humour was his line of elegance, I remember my father saying about Al. My mother's too. Her line of elegance.

The telephone rang and we were told the funeral people had arrived; were we ready for them to come up? I took my mother downstairs and we waited in the courtyard until they had come and gone with their body bag and gurney. Then we came home for dinner, all of us, including Mom, eating the delicious meal of chicken curry that a kind friend had dropped off for us the night before. Jeannie opened the big bottle of fifteen-year-old Glenfiddich she had purchased in the duty-free. Exhaustion descended. I brought out sheets of paper upon which to write the obituary. Al did the job speedily and well. He wrote that Gordon's working life had been invested in the Ontario secondary school system as a teacher, principal and professor of education. Before and after retiring, he was actively involved with the John Howard Society, receiving their National Award for Community Service in 1999. He was survived by his wife of sixty-eight years, Jean née Stevenson, and his four children. My brother went on to name his descendants. "At Gordon's request," he wrote, "no funeral."

Twelve days after Dad died, I had two dreams about him. The first was a bad dream that woke me in the middle of the night. I had been cycling with someone, an impossible route, and my companion was repairing his tire by gluing onto the leak a blue capsule like the sleeping pills my parents took and I also resorted to from time to time. A black car pulled up.

The driver was wearing dark glasses and it was my father, malevolent, middle-aged, coming after me. I had been disobedient. Lying awake, I reassured myself that the thug in dark glasses did not look like Dad. But I felt shaken, horrified actually. I managed to fall asleep again. In the second dream, he appeared as his old self, recognizably so. He was seated rather uncomfortably on a stool in the corner of a bar and beckoned to me affectionately. I went over to him with eagerness. He had that musing, semi-pained look on his face that I knew so well. "What's the matter, Dad?" He gestured to his body and said nothing, but it was obvious that his sorry physical state had continued after death. He was glad to see me, however.

I told Mark about the dreams in the morning as he was getting dressed. "That was an imposter," he said firmly of the first one.

It was what I wanted to hear and I felt better.

SEE YOU TOMORROW EVERY DAY

"WHERE'S GORD?" My mother stood up from the sofa in the lobby and looked around her.

"Mom," I reminded her, "Dad is dead."

"Oh." She paused. "Yes. But where is Gord? I've got track of the other guy. But where is Gord?"

"The other guy. You mean Mark?"

"No, I mean Gord."

"You remember," I said. "He died in September. Three months ago."

"Oh." She paused again. "Yes. I remember."

In her tone there was enough calm resignation that I had the impression she appreciated being set right. My siblings and I had talked it over and agreed that we would always be honest with her and not pretend that Dad wasn't dead. Not lead her on.

I took her upstairs and helped her into her nightgown, and after she brushed her teeth, I tucked her into bed. From her pillow she said, "Now tell me. Are you and Mark sleeping here tonight too?"

"We'll be at home just down the street. We'll be in our house, where we live. And you live here."

Her uncomprehending face.

"You've been living here for almost three years," I said.

"Have I? You mean they know me here?"

"They do."

"Do they? I don't know anybody here. Where will you be tonight? Will you stay over?"

Down the street, in our house, etc.

She said, "And what will happen tomorrow? Someone will come in the morning to get me up."

"Yes, someone will come and get you up and dressed and down for breakfast."

"And where will you be?"

"I'll be at home, just down the street, working at my desk. I'll come to see you in the afternoon about four o'clock."

"You'll come tomorrow?"

"About four."

Her half-comprehending face.

"Mom, do you know where you are?"

"I think so. I'm on the west of the continent . . . and tomorrow I'll move to the other continent. Are we going back to the old land?"

"You're in Ottawa. You're in the Ottawa Valley."

"Well, then, I'm at home," she said.

She was on her ice floe, alone, moving between continents. Dad had gone through the door without her.

She had soldiered on through September and October with a lightened step. I would find her pushing her walker around the perimeter of the residence, the breezes in her hair, her coat unbuttoned. She knew where she was. She managed. She wasn't in despair.

My father had forbidden her from going out on her own, fearing she would get lost. Now she was free and she did not get lost. Not initially. "Well, I went south," she said, when I asked her where she had been, "along the sidewalk out front and then I came back and sat on the sofa and someone brought tea and edibles. Then I thought I could get in by the back door, but I couldn't, so I had to come around again."

She checked in with Dee at the front desk before she went outside and checked in again when she came back. Dee said to me, "She's doing amazingly well. Your father would be so proud of her."

She walked and walked. A bit of ice bobbing in the shipping lanes.

I took to calling her the wild thing. "Have you seen the wild thing?" I would ask Dee when I couldn't find her in her rooms or in the corridors or courtyard. Dee would look up and around, then point, "She's over there." Out of sight behind Colby the caged parakeet, wearing the clothes she always wore, the sweatpants, the oversized fleece jacket. We would go out together and down to Bank Street, then work our way back and around the residence, in through a gate to the courtyard, to a bench in the sun.

I felt grateful to Dad for dying first. How hard it would have been to look after him alone. My mother and I were attuned to each other. We could sit side by side, my arm loosely around her shoulders, and feel peace descend.

Mark said, "She would be happy if she could live outside."

One afternoon I discovered her sitting in my father's green wing chair by the window that overlooked the canal. She said, "I didn't realize what a splendid view he had."

"He hogged the sights for two and a half years," I said.

Another sign of inhibitions falling away was the startling wish she expressed a week after his death. She wanted to see Hurds Lake again, the place my father loved to hate.

"Then we'll go," I said. "We'll go on Saturday."

A year earlier, I had given her a book to peruse of Ottawa Valley photographs. She recognized places in the book and talked about her oldest brother, Harry, taking her and her mother for Sunday drives after church. "Harry was very faithful. We both enjoyed those drives." He owned a pickup truck and during the Depression earned money by transporting groceries for Mr. Flower, the Renfrew grocer who had a neighbouring cottage at the lake.

Dad had said from his wing chair, "Your mother never wanted to go back."

Mom: "Absolute truth."

Dad: "I wonder *why*."

Mom: "I'd have to think about that."

Dad: "There's an *antipathy*." He repeated, "I *wonder why*. She's been all over Ontario but never back to Renfrew."

Mom: "Mother sold the house."

I spoke up then. "There was no one left in Renfrew. Your brothers moved away too."

Dad said, "There was Aunt Em. Your mother left and never went back. Never wanted to go back. You know more about the Valley than she ever did."

I said to my mother, "But you're very fond of the Valley."

"Oh, I am," she said. "I don't know why. I never wanted to go back after my father died. It was the Depression."

Her confusion was showing. She was seven when her father died and she left Renfrew eleven years later.

I didn't say to my father, nor did she suggest, that the reason she never went back was *his* antipathy, not hers—his objection to her family and anything to do with them. He was the reason why she had deprived herself (and her children, for that matter) of the lake that was the solace of her childhood and youth.

We made the drive a week after spreading Dad's ashes at the family cabin. It took an hour to reach Renfrew, and as we drove into town past the fairgrounds, my mother remained silent but alert. On either side of the road were the usual fast-food outlets and new developments that gave her nothing to remember. We bore left on Raglan Avenue and drove south past Thompson Hill, then at Pucker Street we turned right and soon we were on a narrow leafy road that had not changed, not much anyway, since she was a girl. I reminded her of how she used to bicycle this route, the eight miles from Renfrew to the cabin, and she smiled and nodded. We fell under the spell of the wooded approach to the water. The winding dirt road came to a fork, where we bore left, and eventually turned right onto Rocky Lane. We proceeded slowly to the site of Tumble Inn, the name when she was a girl for the converted boathouse of a cabin, now a solid log house, but still simple and rustic.

Relatives of one of her cousins were the owners now. They were there, but they didn't mind us going to the shore-line, where my mother stood leaning on her walker and looking out at the lake. "There's the old island with all its upright trees!" Enraptured, she turned her head and spotted the small white cottage by the water's edge on the right. "And there's Moores'!" All smiles, eagerness, recognition.

In conversation with the owners, who served us tea and cookies, her natural courtesy and enthusiasm helped paper over the slippages in her speech and thoughts. This end of Hurds Lake was both cozy and wild: well-beaten paths meandered under cedars that were allowed to have their way. On the other side of the little inlet, an old man stepped out of the cottage on the point—in my mother's day it had been her Aunt Em's cottage—and the tea-providers identified him as Bill Byers, ninety-two years old.

"Do you know him, Mom?"

"Of course. He was one of the Byers," she said.

On the way home we stopped at the cemetery on Thompson Hill and ate our sandwiches near the Stevenson plot where her mother and father were buried. She perched on her walker in the sunshine, looking around like a curious bird, not entirely registering where she was, yet relaxed and game. I recall the sustained beauty and warmth of those deepening fall days and her composure about Dad. She said she missed him "a whole bunch. I find myself telling him things that have meaning only for us." On the telephone her voice was stronger than it had been for a long time; she identified herself firmly as Jean Hay.

By December her resilience was gone. The weather was unusually mild, with spatters of rain and no snow of any consequence. At the retirement home's Christmas party, held early in the month, an aide took a Polaroid snapshot of my mother posed between Mark and me, which caught for posterity how little of her was left, nothing but scrawny bones and smile. In the melting weather, she melted.

"It's not happening fast enough," she told the doctor. He understood her and enjoyed her succinct way of putting it, but when once again she made her plea that all of her medications be stopped, he again dissuaded her by raising the possibility of a non-fatal stroke. Her mother and one of her brothers had suffered such a lingering and helpless fate. It had always been her greatest fear.

That December "navigation of most exquisite sort" was needed for her to get from her rooms to the hallway, to the elevator, down to the first-floor hallway and around to the dining room and the front desk beyond. Once she spoke of Mark and me living in "your prehistoric abandonment over there." Another time, as I drove her down Aylmer Avenue to our house, she said, "I'm very much impressed by the ruins in your head and how it keeps these places apart."

I tried to imagine what it was like for her not to know where she was. Perhaps a little like being over-edited or badly edited. When an editor changes the word order and punctuation of a sentence, which might be all very well, but you can no longer smell yourself in the sentence, no longer recognize yourself, and it's as if you've been erased and replaced by something altogether foreign—the editor's smell, the editor's mind.

I arrived one day and she was sitting in a chair in the lobby. "Thank goodness you're here," she said, standing up as soon as she saw me. Her head was crowded with a dozen bobby pins, her hair askew and unwashed; she had told the aide that she didn't want a bath, she didn't feel like a bath, a bath every two weeks was enough. She was agitated and I drew her over to the fireplace and we sat down on the sofa. I asked what was the matter.

"Well, Jeannie has died and I tried to reach Dad."

"Mom. Jeannie hasn't died. Only Dad has died. Dad died in September, three months ago. Everyone else in the family is well."

"Oh. All right. Well, I tried to reach Dad on the phone, but I couldn't get through. I didn't have the number."

We went upstairs. I saw her socks under the bedside table. She had bare feet inside her shoes. I got clean socks and put them on her feet. I put Yo-Yo Ma on the CD player for her to listen to. I rubbed her lower legs and walked her through Dad's death and where his ashes were and where hers would go. "Everybody's," she concluded. "We'll be at the lake."

But the applecart would not stay upright. She said again, "I talked to him yesterday on the phone."

By the time we went down to the dining room, she was calmer. I sat with her until her food arrived. She proceeded to give me half of what was on her plate. "It's startling," she said, "how time petered in and petered out this week."

"She's lonely," Mark said later when I told him.

"If things were otherwise, she would live with us," I said. "And I'd be the one losing my mind."

The doctor came and spent half an hour with her, sitting down beside her.

"I'm thinking of my husband," she said to him.

"I know you are," he said.

He explained to her that Dad had been much sicker, much closer to death than she was. "His kidneys stopped working, he had congestive heart failure." Then he said that depression contributed greatly to mental confusion. "Are you depressed?" he asked her.

Long pause. She leaned forward. "What is there to live for?"

I said from across the room, "We have good times together."

"Name one," she said, which made me laugh. I didn't try to name one.

In the end the doctor finally agreed. He said he was "content" to stop all medications, except for sleep and memory, given her consistent and urgent request to let her "beloved vision" come to pass: that is, to let her go.

"Let happen what happens," my mother said.

Death was a completely natural process. What was there to be afraid of?

I brought her home and we watched the best parts of *Easter Parade* together. Fred Astaire doing "Drum Crazy," one of his most ingenious, most breathtaking solos, and my mother a sucker for the drums; then Fred teaching Judy Garland how to dance, hitting their stride with "When That Midnight Choo-Choo Leaves for Alabam"; then "A Couple of Swells"; then another tour-de-force by Fred, backed up by a bevy of dancers: "Steppin' Out with My Baby." For forty-five minutes, nothing could wipe the smiles off our faces. My mother and I were a combined age of 92 + 60 = 152 years old in front of the small screen and we were young again.

"Fred Astaire was truly fabulous," I said with feeling.

"He *was*," she agreed. "It was wonderful to see the old screen actors. It took me back."

After that we sat in the kitchen and ate big pieces of lemon meringue pie. My father had preferred other pies and had had little patience for movies, musicals especially.

Walking to the residence to see Mom alone, I felt relaxed. Still concerned about being late, but much less so. I had a surge of peaceful feelings about my father too. Now he was a character I could recollect in tranquillity. I saw him on his throne of pain, his green wing chair, its bottom as old and sat out as his. An unpeaceful man had found peace, or, more to the point, I had found peace. With his death his disapproval died, or my need for his approval died. Something bad in me had died.

At least for a time. Death and grief smooth things out, but old complications lie in wait.

Substantial amounts of snow fell by Christmas Day. The ploughs were out, the snow thick on cars and rooftops, the bats inside our old walls as agitated as they always were whenever snow fell. Just as children before and during a snowfall become notably restless, active, noisy.

I didn't realize how tired my mother was. Much too tired to stay on for the Christmas pudding. Getting up from the table, her footwork was so slurred that I thought she might be having a stroke. Mark and I got her into the car in the driveway and out of the car at the retirement residence. We put the walker into her hands. For a moment she didn't know what to do with it. "Do I push it forward?" Then upstairs, we helped her out of her clothes and into her bed. I leaned over to kiss her and she raised her head and was all cheekbones and smile and silvery-white falling-back hair.

The next day, I called her in the morning to say I would pick her up in half an hour and bring her home for lunch.

"And what about Gord?"

I said nothing for a moment. "You remember about Dad."

"Oh," she said. "Yes."

"So I'll come and get you. Sochi leaves later this afternoon. We can have lunch together."

"Is Dad dead?"

"Yes."

Out walking a few days later, she told me she had been tipping her hat to her mother recently, appreciating more what it must have been like to be widowed at forty-two. "All the weight falling on the one person. All the aloneness on her skull." We saw children in a long line crossing the street and she spoke of them moving through "the snow-flocked air." Flecks of snow, a flock of children, the look and texture of flocked wallpaper. We walked a fair distance, keeping to the street as she pushed her walker through the snow and slush. Then we sat on the metal bench in the sunshine outside the residence. There was warmth in the sun and the beauty of glinting snow-dust shaken off various mops: trees, bushes, rooftops, like gold dust falling through the air.

But she was so discouraged. "Life is a nonplus, let's say," was how she put it. And inside, after checking the mail, she wanted to sit down. She had something to say.

"Tell me," she said, as I knelt beside her chair in the lobby, "when am I going to stop feeling sorry for myself?"

"Are you feeling sorry for yourself?"

"I am. And it's so unhelpful."

"You don't take it out on anyone," I said.

She shifted to the subject of the doctor and what he might give her to end it.

"You have to be sick," I said. "You have to be in pain. He has to have a reason to give you something. You told him you weren't in pain."

"I'm in pain in my head," she said.

Tears fall, wrote Al in reply to one of my emails about her.

Jeannie remarked when we spoke on the telephone, "Every time I call to talk with Mom, I hear her voice a wee bit smaller."

In the middle of January I got a call from one of the nurses saying that my mother had cut her hair and put something pink in it. They had taken away the scissors.

I went over and found her stretched out on the chester-field in her room. Her hair looked much the same and there was no longer any trace of pink. Whatever it was, I never did learn. She said, "I've been ruminating about your dad and whether there's a condition in which we might see each other again." She said she didn't suppose there was, but it was pleasant to think about.

Throughout January the snow continued, broken by intervals of rain. One afternoon she said that her body was "assorting itself to die." She had spent the day lying in bed, she said. "That sort of desolation."

Did her body feel different, I asked, or was this in her head?

She said it was from the waist up. "What will you do?" she asked. "Will there be a burial?"

I said we would do what we had done with Dad: first cremation, then spreading the ashes at the lake. She didn't remember, and so I took her through the Saturday following his death, how we drove to the lake in two cars and once we got there we put her in a wheelchair. How Al and his son Phil lifted her in the chair over the wildly uneven ground with much joshing and hilarity amongst the three of them, how we made a fire and roasted hotdogs and drank scotch, how we planted a small white spruce and spread his ashes around it, how Stu spoke movingly and well, wishing Dad bon voyage but at the same time urging him to grow roots here, in this place he had loved, and how he was a good man, who could be gruff, but an honourable man.

"I hadn't remembered," she said. "I guess it got lost in the gloom."

The next time I brought her home, I showed her photographs from that September day five months earlier, and she was happy to be looking at them, recognizing the place and all the faces of her family, and she ate prodigiously. But we had been late with supper and by the time we finished it was eight o'clock. Her path from kitchen to bathroom was laboured, even more so from bathroom to hallway. I had to hold her up.

On her walker, inside the retirement home, she moved normally again beside Mark and me. But in her room she stood lost, exhausted. "What do I do?"

I started to undress her, and as she sat on the chesterfield she collapsed into herself and began to weep. Holding her, "Mom, what's wrong?"

"It's rough," she said.

She was too exhausted to brush her teeth. I led her to her bed, got her lying down and held her again. "There are good times and there are hard times," she said.

"Do you have everything you need?"

"Everything I need," she answered, and she thanked us repeatedly for all that we had done.

The nurse came in with her sleeping pill and gave it to her with a glass of water, after which Mark tucked her in, smoothed the blankets, kissed her cheek. We went to the door and put our boots back on, then paused in the doorway to look back at her and wave good night. "Sleep well, Mom." She was lying on her side and she smiled her beautiful smile, and waved back at us.

I was full of grief. Premature grief, perhaps. Or grief-in-anticipation. Or just plain grief.

She continued to surprise and delight me with her poetic twists and turns. Looking around at the deep snow before climbing the steps to our front porch, she said, "The snow is puissant." It was such a sophisticated French word to roll off her tongue—she who didn't speak French—that I searched for it later in the *Oxford English Dictionary* and there it was, meaning mighty, powerful. One morning, as I left after a visit, she said to me with a smile, "Good luck with all your in luck things," a turn of phrase that made me feel selected for nothing but the best luck. Of the wide-open yellow and red tulips on our kitchen table, she exclaimed, "Those are the prettiest Brazilian troubadours I've ever seen." When I told her we had spotted our first robin at the foot of the garden, she lit up and said, "Spring has arrived by the throat."

And on the telephone one morning, "I am a bit muzzled up, a little bit underfed. I'm not sure where I am. Things are looking more familiar now that I'm inside. I've seen this place before from the outside." She described herself in relation to her mind as being "not upstairs-fit."

"You've got a lot to do that we don't have to do," she said to me once. "So go hit it, kid."

And another time, by way of parting, "See you tomorrow every day."

She was receptive to some of the poems I read to her and not others; receptive to Robert Frost, but not to Wallace Stevens. With Frost there was a lot for her to grab on to, physical detail and ready emotion and unbegrudging rhyme. Reading Wallace Stevens, on the other hand, was like trying to enter a rich man's house.

I went to get her one afternoon to take her to the Baroque concert at the church on the corner, and she was standing with her walker looking out the window of her room. I greeted her from the door and she turned and gave me her usual heartfelt, "Thank God you're here."

We moved toward each other. "How are you?" I asked.

Her face was full of emotion. "I'm lost," she said simply. And she began to weep, a dry weeping. I put my arms around her and her body shook.

I got her to sit on the chesterfield and sat down beside her and put my arms around her again, and she was like an ancient child weeping—lost and weeping. "Where am I?"

I told her where she was. "Where did you think you were?"

"Oh, I'm in many places. Where I am keeps changing."

We walked to the elevator and she said, "I've got some of my wits. But not all."

And then there was the day she said, "I've had a good life, all things consoled."

The instinct to make art had abandoned her, but not the instinct to save food. She could not pass the communal fruit bowl in the lobby without her hand reaching out like a raccoon's for apples and oranges, which she slipped into the basket of her walker and wheeled to her room. We took to calling her the fruit tree, self-grafting, everbearing. Anything not eaten at mealtime she wrapped in a napkin and took back to her room. Her little fridge groaned with what she salted away. Every few days I emptied it out into a canvas bag, assuring her that nothing would go to waste. Then I would stop by the kitchen on my way out of the building and put the food in the garbage and the napkins into the laundry bag and the plates on the counter. I stopped at the famous fruit bowl and returned apples and oranges.

While my father was still alive, they used to eat some of these leftovers with their afternoon tea. I would arrive and there might be three bowls filled with chopped-up oranges, apples, sausage, cheese, bread, whatever she had rescued from the dining room, all prepared against expected company. Dad would say, "She'll want that heated." So I would put two bowls in the microwave and take them out steaming and carry them into the living room, where my parents would tuck in. Depending on what was on offer and depending on my mood, I would or would not partake. I remember slices of bacon, pieces of muffin, more banana, bits of chicken, all mixed up, and thinking as I ate the combination that it wasn't bad. But then my mother had raised me not to be a fussy eater.

From time to time, I joined her for dinner in the dining room. Once, dessert was strawberry ice cream with an éclair so small you needed a jeweller's glass to see it, as the wry gentleman at the next table remarked. I didn't want my dessert, so my mother took my ice cream (in her old age she was a glutton for ice cream) and gave me her éclair. Then when she saw I hadn't touched either of the éclairs, she prevented the waiter from taking them away. She drew the plate close and said to them tenderly, "Don't worry. I'll look after you."

One day, toward the end, I found a folded napkin holding something soft in her sweater pocket. Inside was a scoop of melted chocolate ice cream.

Winter gave way to spring. My mother on the back porch removed her sweater and sat like Huck Finn in sunhat and white shirt, soaking her feet in a basin of hot water as goldfinches came to the feeder a few yards away. In my comings and goings I kept seeing neighbours taking down Christmas lights and bringing out bicycles. The last patch of snow vanished from our garden. Snowdrops—a cluster of them—poked up at the edge of the lower garden steps. Two crocuses blossomed near the fence. Mark worked in the garden and swabbed the winter's dirt off the back porch. He set up a birdhouse, hoping to coax a pair of swallows to take up residence. We opened windows and the smell of the outside poured in. To walk upstairs was like burying my face in sheets dried in the wind.

From the second floor, leaning out my window, I saw how beautiful the lines and levels of the garden were. There were no embellishments, no blossoms (the few crocuses and snowdrops were invisible from here), just rich duns and russets, stone-wall outlines, bare cherry, whitish lavender, pearly-grey lamb's ears, the dark wet earth, the ripe-green ground cover, the lovely gradual downhill slope. A child could run down it and not lose her balance. A two-year-old could do it.

What happened next happened in two stages, like a bell tolling twice. The head nurses brought me in and asked me if I thought it was safe for my mother to go on walks by herself. In the milder March weather she was heading out frequently without telling anyone, so no one knew where she was. I couldn't say it was safe. They said they would hate to see her hit by a car or sprawled in a ditch. They suggested having one of the aides take her for a walk in the afternoon, and that I come later, after supper, about five thirty, to take her out again and then settle her down afterwards. As to what lay ahead—further loss of mobility to accompany the loss of her mind so that she ended up vacant in a chair—they could not say. It was impossible to tell. They were glad that she had not elected to stop eating, "which would be horrible," they said.

More horrible than this? It struck me that it takes as long to die in some cases as it does to get through school. My father had been lucky, the doctor said in one of our frank conversations, to still have the wits to engineer his own exit.

The bell tolled a second time toward the end of March. They brought me in again and this was the meeting when I was told it was no longer safe for my mother to be anywhere but "inside." That is, on the locked side of the second floor.

Their "memory unit."

All this I had been prepared for, in the sense that I had known it was probably coming. But it shell-shocked and grieved me no less.

In our kitchen the previous Sunday, Mom had said, "See I was getting back into town because Mark was coming back. Hard stuff. We might as well leave it apart. It was the end—we'll skip the whole thing. I just don't remember. I do not remember. When I was in training and I went out to Lizzie, I would get the odd meal. I never thought of that as unusual having full day meals, morning, noon and night. Well, I remember how this started up and that we'd go in and if we were doing an opera dish—I have no real memory of it so I shouldn't go on about it. Darned things happen to you when you lose your ecclesiastical mind. How was it I got hooked into knowing more about John North? It was a long time ago. I don't think I can make it clearer than I've already made it. I'm all worn out, that's the whole thing. I give up!"

It used to be enough for me to look her in the eye and wait, and she would recall Dad's death and realize she had forgotten. But on that Sunday and again the next day, she did not believe me. When I persisted (she had been walking in the hall and wouldn't come outside with me until she had found him), it was as if I had delivered a body blow: the double fact of his death and her forgetfulness. How did it happen? How did he die? And how could she have forgotten? "I feel like sitting down and weeping," she said, pushing her walker in front of her, half bent over, as if ploughing a field at the end of a long, long day.

It had reached the point where pretending was simpler and kinder, better than my mother having to relive Dad's death as a new piece of information over and over again, in what was nothing less than water torture. I asked the doctor what we might say to her instead. He suggested an evasion that was not a lie. That we tell her Dad was not here *yet*. And that's how we phrased it from then on.

For me the locked unit was the end of the world. To get through the door you had to use an access code. The hallway and rooms on the other side were agreeable enough, not that different from the rest of the building, though each room was identified not only by a name but by a picture of its inhabitant, so the lost could find their way home. That was the idea, except my mother did not recognize herself in the photograph we tacked up, and why would she recognize her happy eighty-eight-year-old self? In the common room there were long tables at which people sat, many in wheelchairs, most of them half-toppled from brain loss and bone loss. To my horror I recognized some of them. They used to inhabit the open floors and I had forgotten all about them. I recognized Margaret, the one my father loved to hate, seated at the end of a table, eyes closed, grinding her teeth, fattened up by feeding. Her intrusive voice was intact, her English accent unchanged, as she muttered away to herself.

So you could stop all of your medications and still wind up shipwrecked on these barren shores.

We moved my mother's furnishings into her new room. She was doing chair exercises with the others in the common room and saw us and waved as Mark and I trucked loads over on a dolly, back and forth. Only later did she come to the room and approve. She lay down on the chesterfield and napped as we continued to hang her paintings on the walls. I said to her after she woke up that everything was on one floor now; she wouldn't have to bother with the elevator anymore. "Very good," she said.

When I returned to take her for a walk, I found her with Murphy the therapy dog, "who looks just like Jet," she said, delighted with him, offering him water out of a paper cup. In general, however, her spirits were much lower. I took her outside to see the crocuses and she confessed, "I feel like I'm in two halves." Again she spoke of Dad's death, for the fact of it had sunk in and mutilated her.

Over the next few days, she grew calmer. The closed unit and the extra attention seemed to relax her. I cautioned her that she should shut her door and let it lock behind her whenever she left her room, since attendants had warned about other residents wandering in and walking off with things or lying down on her bed, though not intentionally, I added.

"So it's accidental," she said, with one of her flashes of insight and lucidity, "not wilful petulance."

On April Fool's Day we had big snowflakes mixed with rain. Upstairs, at my desk, I listened to Mark on the back porch pump up the tires of his bicycle. Every morning I heard the pump going up and down as he rushed, always late, for work. His willingness to patch and repatch endlessly the inner tubes of his tires made me marvel. As my father had said many, many years ago, shaking his head at the difference between them, "He has the patience of Job."

I knew Mark had packed his lunch and it included radishes. He was as devoted to radishes as his brother Lexi had been to dill pickles.

People live on and on, I thought, thinning themselves out, until you can see right through them. Except for those who don't, like Lexi, who died in his fifties.

The day before, Mark and I had gone for a long walk

through the arboretum to the grove of magnolias. The tallest held their just-bursting buds up into the evening light, where they shimmered like white gold. I thought of my parents' wedding bands, exchanged in wartime, on May 17th, 1943. My mother must have been thinking of those years of dark uncertainty when she remarked, pushing her walker into the wind one day, "Every generation thinks they're heading into a taciturn time."

In early April we left Ottawa to spend a week with Ben in Spain, where he was teaching English to rural schoolchildren. My brothers would stay with Mom in our absence.

Ben had discovered that he enjoyed teaching children and was good at it. Often he left school at the end of the day feeling exhausted but satisfied. "I invite them to laugh at me and I'm generous in my compliments." His pleasure filled me with joy and I wanted to tell Dad. After his death, I had found in my father's filing cabinet a folder prepared by his history class in Guelph the year we returned from England: *The Best 100 "Great Quotations" as said by G. Hay. 1967–68.* Among which:

> —*Turn directly to your notes, all other books away and off your desks.*
> —*Read us what you have and we'll tee off from there.*
> —*You've known that ever since you fell out of your cradle.*
> —*What is fraternité—well, sister, you should know.*
> —*Where's your book, bub.*
> —*Hard to get the dog-team started this morning, isn't it???*
> —*Chamberlain said, "Hitler missed the bus." Actually, it was Chamberlain who missed it.*
> —*The Arabs claim they were in Palestine long before*

Joshua ever came romping around.
—Great guts!!!
—Solomon may know; Hay doesn't.

That was him all right, though with more verve and gusto than I had ever given him credit for.

We arrived home from Spain on the night of April 18th, a Wednesday. Coming through the door near midnight, I was surprised that Stu was still here, though asleep. I had assumed he would be back in Montreal, knowing we were on our way. His shoes were in the hallway. Lights were on in the living room. His work was on the dining room table. But there was no note.

We went to bed and slept. At six I got up and put on my bathrobe and went down into the kitchen to make coffee. Stu joined me half an hour later, coming into the kitchen in his slippers, to tell me in his low-key way that Mom was near the end. She was comatose, he said. She had fallen ill on Saturday, seemed to be somewhat better on Monday, but then had slid right down. It was pneumonia.

Mark joined us and Stu gave him the news. I stood rooted to the spot, holding my coffee mug against my chest. How could it have happened so fast? And why hadn't Stu left us a note so that we could have spent the night with her? And why wasn't I racing over there right now to be with her?

Because I didn't want to go. I felt myself in the grip of a cowardly shying away, a paralysis that made me ask myself how much love I really felt.

So it wasn't until a few minutes after seven that we directed our steps to the residence, walking the familiar route up Aylmer Avenue. In her room on the second floor, she was indeed lying comatose, an air tube in her nostrils, the noise of the air machine pervading the room. I took her hand and spoke to her, but she did not respond. Her eyes were closed. Her breaths were rapid with a little rattling sound in her throat. Debbie came in, the head nurse for the second floor, a small woman, in her late thirties, experienced and reliable, a very good nurse. "Thank God you're here," she said to me in an echo of my mother's old refrain. She took me into the hallway and explained that she didn't think my mother would outlast her shift, which ended in the early afternoon.

I returned to Mom's bedside. Stu and Mark and I sat with her for about an hour, at which point Mark left to go home and put in a load of laundry. Debbie had already come in and removed the air tube and shut off the loud machine, since it was doing no good, and checked my mother's fingers. "See how blue they are, the fingertips? That's one of the signs that she doesn't have long left."

I was holding my mother's hand, we were looking at the small photo album Stu had found on the table in my study, with its many small snaps of our grandparents, of Dad and his sister and brother, of close family friends, including Uncle Hugh, all together at West Hill where my father had grown up. "That's how it was," Stu was saying. "I don't suppose you have the memories of it that I do." And Mom stopped breathing. We turned to look at her, transfixed. About fifteen or twenty seconds went by. The vein in her neck pulsed strongly, visibly. Her mouth was open. Then she took a deep gulping breath. Ten seconds went by, then another breath. A series of these gulping, racking breaths, perhaps fifteen of them, enough that I wanted them to stop. "Apnea," said Stu. Was it at this point that I leaned over and said in her ear, "We love you, Mom"? A little earlier, perhaps. And now, "We love you, Mommy." And at what exact point did Stu come around the other side of the bed? He put his hands on her shoulders and said, "You can let go now."

The vein continued to pulse after the last ragged intake of breath. We stayed watching and gradually the pulse stopped. It was 8:47 a.m., April 19th, 2012.

Only after that did I go in search of Debbie. She was in the dining area standing next to a woman who had choked on her food, striking her back to expel whatever had lodged. I touched Debbie on the shoulder. She turned and I said, "She's gone." She looked at me with all the sympathy an excellent nurse can muster, until she was diverted back to the old woman, who had just showered the table with a flood of food.

The doctor came. He gave me a sympathetic hug. Then he asked me how the wine was in Spain, which made me laugh. What a good doctor he was. He checked my mother and said he would do the paperwork.

Stu and I were alone with her again. The window was open. Birdsong and sunshine poured in. At some point Debbie stuck her head in the door to say the cremation people were on the telephone. When did we want them to come? Noon, I said.

There was the problem, and mystery, of her oblong wedding ring, which would not come over the knuckle. My mother or one of the aides must have squeezed the soft gold into a shape that would not slip off. Stu went into the bathroom and got soap and lathered her finger and worked the ring off.

Her breath all this time had been sweet. No hint of sourness—the sourness I often held away from a little when I sat beside her. I used to make sure she brushed her teeth with toothpaste whenever I was with her in the evening. Not a hint of sourness on her breath.

Stu left to go back to the house to do something for his stiff neck and Mark met him on the way. Then Mark was with me and Mom. He spoke to her, wished her well.

And now her body began to cool. First her nose got cold, her forehead cooled, her chin. Then her cheeks were cool when I pressed mine against hers. Her earlobe was soft and folded into itself, something between a petal and a mushroom. I smelled her hair. Not then, but later, I thought to cut a lock of it. I folded it up inside a piece of paper. Then I thought to cut a lock for my sister and folded it up the same way. Her fingers were bluish and no longer curled around mine. I remembered a friend saying how strange it was to hold her mother's hand and not receive an answering squeeze. Her fingers lay flat and long.

The cooling. Her feet got cold. Bluish. Her toes were curled under, unlike Dad's. The nurses had said how peaceful she looked when they came in to move her from her side onto her back, and to position a pillow under her head. I didn't think so, not especially peaceful. She looked strained to me, the struggle to breathe still on her face. But over the course of the next three hours her expression smoothed and so did her skin. The blood drained from her lips. And—this was Mark's noticing—her open mouth and sagging jaw, which Stu had tried unsuccessfully to close, closed on their own, drew imperceptibly up, so that by the end her lips were only slightly parted. Later, writing to a friend, I mentioned how she had always been ashamed of her teeth: perhaps posthumous vanity was at play.

Her cheekbones became more pronounced.

How little she was, Mark remarked. What would she have weighed? Ninety pounds?

The beautiful day poured in.

The hairs on her chin. Only a few weeks before I had plucked the worst offenders, not that there were many. She was not bewhiskered the way so many old women are. I thought of using the tweezers both while she was dying and after she was dead, and let it go.

The two undertakers arrived, the same ones that had come for Dad, a stocky woman with a natural manner and a stocky man with an unnatural manner. They wrapped her in a sheet, lifted her into the unzipped red body bag on the trolley, leaving her head wrapped but her face uncovered. They asked if we were done before covering the face and zipping up the bag, buckling her on, and wheeling her out the door. Then the man came back to ask sheepishly for the elevator code.

That afternoon Mark and I went for a long walk in the arboretum. In the ash grove we saw two hawks perched high in separate trees. A pair of tough old birds, reunited. Samuel Beckett's bony, beaky face came to mind and his directive that his simple granite gravestone should be any colour, "so long as it's grey." We walked to the magnolia grove, catching it at its glorious peak, and around the corner came Jeremiah Bartram and his small and dapper dog, Maximilian. It was almost like meeting Moses. He was someone I had seen perhaps twice in a dozen years, a deeply religious man whose parents had lived around the corner from my parents in London. He had always spoken so warmly of my mother and father. We told him that my mother had died that very morning and he was full of sympathy. He said he would pray for my mother, and for me and Mark, whom he called Brian. The glitch in his memory made me smile. Nothing felt sombre. My mother had taken flight. We walked home under more flowering trees, the plums all in bloom, and butterflies in the blossoms.

Now the neighbourhood was a village of memories. I crossed the bridge and again saw Dad coming toward me in his shorts and old-man legs. I passed the big boulder under the climbing tree at Southminster Church and saw them seated on it, side by side, resting. I had the physical memory of helping my mother up and down our front steps. Of helping my father without it appearing that I was. I remembered the car ride every Sunday between the residence and our house, getting her into the car, buckling her in, hoisting the walker into the trunk, driving past the brick houses and up the slope to the residence, then along its curving driveway. I recalled the day I drove up Aylmer Avenue and saw her by herself, pushing her walker on the sidewalk, in her red knit sweater and mint-green mittens. I recalled bringing her water lilies from the lake, how she quoted her mother's view that you can't cut water lilies and have them keep. "They don't have the troops inside," she had said. I recalled sitting with her dead and cooling body as April sunshine poured into her room. I can still feel the heat on my hand from her lower neck, below the nape, and feel her cool forehead under my cheek. A snow-bank is warmest where it meets the ground.

Even now, whenever I pass the retirement residence, I look at its facade and think, You escaped, Mom. And so have I.

THE FOOD OF LOVE

LIVING WITH MY MOTHER: the number of times I think of her every day and the reasons. Whenever I use a rubber spatula to scrape the last particle of food out of a dish. And whenever I don't.

Whenever I bake something in the oven—only one thing, rather than several at a time, and let all that heat go to waste.

Whenever I open the refrigerator and dally for a moment, unable to put my hand on what I need, letting cold air escape.

Whenever I peel roots—potato, carrot, yucca, malanga, batata—and my hand goes numb around the peeler as it does around a pencil.

Whenever I look at my hands: the squareness, the skin tone, the freckles, the big knuckles, the pronounced veins. Whenever I grip a pen or pencil before starting to write.

Whenever I whip on what I wore the day before—undershirt, blouse, sweater—in one fell swoop, layer inside layer having rested overnight on the back of a chair.

Whenever I smell lipstick and recall hers, a bit of red in the bottom of a tube, probed with a matchstick tipped with a twist of cotton batten, applied with the same.

Whenever I walk a long distance rather than take the bus.

Whenever I take offence. Her touchiness flickers in my mind, although over the years she acquired more easiness, gradually but tellingly, like the hair on Samson's head.

Whenever I crack open an egg and with my fingertip wipe all the egg white out of the shell into the bowl.

Whenever it's cold, I imagine the defiant temperature of her hands. "Oh, they were just in cold water." And the layer upon layer of clothing.

Whenever it's hot, I imagine her wilting.

One humid evening in June of 2000, I was making her a lemon meringue pie. She and my father were arriving the next day, and as I worked at the stove I wondered if the pie would turn out, and whether she would be the more pleased if it did or if it didn't. It was much too warm to be baking anything, but the lemon filling would cool overnight, I would make the roast in the morning before the day's heat began, bake the pastry shell at the same time, then in the afternoon, before going to the airport, I would assemble the pie and slather on the meringue and bake it at 425 degrees for five minutes.

To my mind a lemon meringue pie was the supreme act of love. Whenever my mother wanted to outdo herself on someone's behalf, she constructed one. But acts of love are never uncomplicated, and this act, complicated in itself since I hadn't made such a pie in years, was further bedevilled by what I imagined my mother's reaction would be.

She liked a soft filling, just as she liked only the freshest corn and the most perfect golden-brown toast. Fastidious about those few select items, forgiving and protective about anything else related to food. I stood at the stove stirring. I had measured three tablespoons of cornstarch and three tablespoons of flour into the top of a double boiler, mixed them with one and a half cups of sugar, then added, slowly, one and a half cups of boiling water. I had consulted three cookbooks, but even without the cookbooks I knew that all-important was the stirring. A quiet evening and lovely to be alone in the nervous prelude to the next day's visit. Would my mother feel puzzled, criticized, chafed by the trouble I was taking? Was I, in creating her favourite pie and possibly doing it better than she ever had, one-upping her, and would she be mildly irked and say something like, "Well, God bless you," but in less than ringing tones? Would she see in this overlong effort not a tribute to her but a daughter showing off? Would it be better, in other words, to make not a good pie but a dud?

I stirred at the stove and stirred myself up, alternately entranced by how the ingredients thickened and became smooth, and harassed by old history. Vivid in my mind was the previous December, when looking out my kitchen window, I had seen a white elevator descend from the sky and stop at every level: treetop, rooftop, car top, hedge, bush, ground. The sight of snow covering every damp surface had given me courage and peace of mind, and I had telephoned my mother and asked her to promise me something. On the wall beside the telephone were several family photographs and while the phone rang three, four, five times, my eyes rested on the wedding photo taken more than fifty years earlier when my mother was a very pretty woman of twenty-three. It was a photograph I knew well, having studied it as a child, completely bewildered because the mother I knew was not the least bit pretty. Where had her prettiness gone? There had been a ripeness to her face, an expectant fullness and a sweetness, and no sign at all of tension or fatigue or ill temper. She wasn't wearing her glasses and her mouth was closed, which helped, since her teeth were not good, for which reason she forbade candy to all of her children. "I ate candy without restraint and look at my teeth. Do you want teeth like mine?" Candy was sinful (though not the sugar in her own desserts, the cakes that didn't always rise, the pies whose pastry could be tough, the runny custards and rice puddings that made me gag; not her own desserts that ran the gauntlet from horrible to sublime, since she also made cream puffs and apple dumplings, and one memorable time, Bavarian cream. But candy—candy was sinful).

It was on the subject of food for Christmas that I made my telephone call. First, I told her what food I was bringing: dinner and dessert for Boxing Day, and the stollen I always made for Christmas breakfast, using my ex-mother-in-law's recipe for the yeast-raised sweet bread. Then I made my plea. "It's Christmas, Mom. If there's too much food, promise you won't worry. It doesn't matter. It really doesn't matter."

"All right," she said, but her voice had the high note rising-to-thinness that it got whenever she was nettled but wanted you to think she wasn't. No doubt my voice had its usual pushy, critical edge, though people have always said they could not tell my voice apart from hers.

It was an earlier conversation that had set me to brooding and pleading about Christmas (always a collaborative endeavour, with my mother making the big meal on Christmas Day and the rest of us taking care of the Eve and Boxing Day). During this earlier call she had instructed me not to bring too much. "We won't be able to eat it," she said. "There's always too much food." Then she said, "What I make will be plain, because"—and this she added in no uncertain terms—"we don't need rich food."

So it began, the paring away of pleasure down to the bare bones of "quite enough."

Yet I knew she loved Christmas. It was her favourite holiday as a child in Renfrew when for dessert they had either green jello or red. The colour alternated with the location. If it had been red at her widowed mother's, it would be green at her Aunt Em's. Every year, no matter who carved the turkey, as the youngest child my mother got the neck. She claimed she didn't mind, except for the vein down the middle, which reminded her of a worm. "Turkey is turkey, and it was good."

I wanted her to mind. To mind very much.

The above-mentioned Aunt Em lived with her unmarried brother George and their invalid sister Maggie. If Christmas was at their small house on Lochiel Street, then after dinner Aunt Em would wrap several slices of turkey breast in wax paper and slip the package into my mother's pocket. This treasure my mother would put on the kitchen windowsill at home to keep cool and eat at her leisure, sharing it with Mickey the cat. Well, sometimes she said she shared it, sometimes she claimed she kept it all to herself, not even sharing with her cat. The fluidity of the telling never bothered me. For Christmas her gift from the two aunts and Uncle George was always the same, a hand-knit pair of mittens with a quarter in one thumb. "A middling present," was her verdict, "neither lavish nor stingy."

As a parent her attitude toward Christmas was a throwback to all of that Depression-era making-do.

I proceeded to add small spoonfuls of the thickened filling to the bowl of four beaten egg yolks (my mother would have used no more than three, probably two, but having cut back on the cornstarch, I increased the eggs), and is any colour more enchanting than the pale lemon yellow of yolks beaten to within an inch of their lives? I stirred rapidly so the yolk wouldn't cook into solid bits, then poured the smooth mixture back into the double boiler and kept stirring—now it was crucial to stir without a break—for another ten minutes, before I removed the pan from the heat, added lemon juice, one third of a cup, and the grated rind of one lemon, and a generous whack of butter.

Well, it wasn't the least bit thick. Perhaps overnight, as it cooled, it would thicken.

No such luck. The next morning, I explored its soupiness with a spoon. Dear cookbook writers, dear *Fucking Joy of Fucking Cooking*, you make a serious mistake when you tell us to add lemon juice *after* removing the pan from the heat; all that does is liquefy the filling.

I set about recooking and did not spare the cornstarch horses. Already it was sunny and hot, so I turned on the ceiling fan and my thoughts slid back to the summer years before, when my mother in a very public display of love made a lemon meringue pie for my two uncles visiting from the United States, Uncle Al and Uncle Chuck, the husband of my father's sister. We were living in Guelph then, miles away from the cool mornings and cool evenings of my childhood beside the water. I was sixteen. My mother suffered in the heat. Her feet swelled, and her legs too, and in the evening, after the dishes were done, she used to sink into an armchair and rest her aching calves and ankles on an upholstered stool. In those days she was heavier, by no means fat, not even plump, but she was carrying extra weight. I remember her taking the roll of middle-aged thigh that bulged out her pedal-pushers (capris we call them now) that were faded golden in colour with a matching sleeveless top. With both hands she squeezed the spill of flesh, horrified yet sufficiently entertained that she burst out laughing. I, too, was heavier in those days. From that summer no pictures of me remain looking like a sausage in a white shift because I tore them up.

That was the summer many relatives descended. From England came my great-aunt Muriel with her bowlegs, her enormous crooked nose that turned black in the cold, her rakish blue eyeshadow, her amber cigarette holder. From the States, as I say, arrived my two newly widowed uncles and their two sons. I wonder now where everyone slept. Our rented house had four bedrooms upstairs, one of which my father used as his study, but where we all bedded down and whether I gave up my room to my great-aunt, I can't remember. The nephews would have slept in the basement. But were the two bereaved uncles also consigned to the basement, while the household that had never known grave misfortune hummed along above their heads?

In the middle of their weeklong visit to us, the uncles and nephews drove to Toronto for the day. In their absence my mother relaxed, a lowering of the guard so sumptuous and welcome that my own muscles loosen as I write these words. She still had Auntie Muriel on her hands, but the pace and demands eased off. After lunch she washed her hair and put it in curlers, as she used to do in the 1950s and '60s, and then she began to make the pie. She should have known better. A lemon meringue pie commenced in the afternoon will never set by dinner.

I think it fair to say that in all her years my mother never let a store-bought cookie into the house, unless imported by a guest in an act of thoughtless thoughtfulness, a contradiction that meets its match in her demanding generosity. My mother was making the pie out of love, yes, but also because she hoped to be praised. Above the bubbling of the lemon filling, she expected, and had every right to expect, sustained applause.

That night she sat at her end of the dinner table, nearest the kitchen, my father sat at the other end, and the rest of us in between. Her curlers were visible under a bilious-yellow net scarf that had drifted into her possession from who knows where, and though she was doing her best to hide them, her strained feelings were also on view in the slight movements and adjustments of her tightened lips. For in front of my father, lording it over her pie, was a garish, thickly iced triple-layer cake from a bakery in Toronto. A gift from my uncles.

The uncle by marriage, the one who drove a Cadillac and loved brass bands and was the fire chief for his small town in upper New York State, was singing the praises of the Holiday Inn because "you always know what you're getting." His bald head flaked, his eyes were pink, his teeth bad. Nobody in my family knew why my father's sister had married Chuck Sweeney except for the usual reason of sheer desperation. She had died the previous spring. After her death, her fifty-six-year-old body underwent an autopsy that revealed the organs of an eighty-year-old woman. This marvel of nature was of special interest to me, for in my sluggishness I had drawn from my parents many a dig about my resemblance to my aunt. She had been a girl, according to my scathing father, who could not get her bottom off the ground. That she had aged on the inside far more than on the outside struck me as a satisfactorily morbid fate.

The other uncle, the favourite uncle, my father's brother, had an inexplicable fondness for Uncle Chuck. By rights, my uncle Al, a principled pacifist, should not have been able to abide Uncle Chuck, who was a champion of the war in Vietnam and an unashamed Republican. It was a lesson, I think now, in the straight and narrow of affinity and affection. There is no straight and narrow. Maybe Uncle Al found it a relief to be in the company of so gregarious and unabashed a man. It took no effort. There was no understated, ardent, shy and diffident love he had to deal with. You could be coarse, crass, genial, frivolous. You could even watch TV, which you could not do in our house. We didn't have one.

My father said once, "Al trusts Chuck to do things he trusts no one else to do." There was naked wonder in his voice and wistfulness.

Over dinner the two uncles conversed across the table, while my mother chewed and chewed, and my father, as usual first to the finish line, sat quietly, never having much to say but always the one in charge of carving the meat and serving the dessert.

Predictably, heartbreakingly, the pie was runny. Its yellow guts spilled wide on the plate when my father served it with his usual dexterity, holding his tongue but not containing the exasperation that spread across his face. There were few takers. Except for my mother and father, everyone was seduced by the competition. I remember the silence that greeted my mother's pie, the unforgivable silence, though at the time all I really felt was embarrassment.

Those uncles. I could kill them now.

At four o'clock I left the house for the airport, too nervous and clumsy to manage a simple hair elastic. My hair blew into my eyes and I rolled up the window and recalled again the colour of the net scarf my mother wore over her curlers the day her pie was spurned—an awful shade of butterscotch and lime. Under the scarf her face wore the controlled disappointment typical of tired women everywhere. And I realized that I had not prepared a pie for her at all. I had prepared a test.

Not an act of love, but a test of love. This seemed neither kind nor fair, and it occurred to me that I should warn her, so she wouldn't be startled into making the wrong remark in the kitchen.

At the airport I parked the car and headed across the steamy lot to the air-conditioned arrivals area, and there they were, beside the conveyor belt of rolling luggage. My father bald and still very erect, my mother tiny and stooped with abundant white hair, both of them leaning forward, still hale and hearty. I watched them for a moment before going forward. They had gym bags over their shoulders and were dressed in faded florals. My father's shirt looked Hawaiian, my mother's dress like a shift from the 1960s. They would be staying only one night with me, then continuing on to Pangnirtung on Baffin Island, where for a week they would rent a room in someone's house, the friend of a friend. (One of the paintings the trip inspired is on the wall downstairs, a scene of the bay with a solitary iceberg and a single rowboat floating on its blue waters.)

I called to them. They looked up, still thinking about their luggage, not wanting to miss it as it went by, and smiled broadly as I went forward and we embraced.

It was all so easy. My nervousness disappeared. It was gone.

On our way to the car, I told them with a droll smile that I had worked myself to the bone preparing for their arrival, but neither one heard me. The airport was noisy. Both of them were a little deaf.

At home they followed me into the kitchen, which faced west into the hot afternoon sun. The blinds were lowered, the room shadowy. I asked them if they would like tea or a cold beer, and then I pointed to the pie on the counter. "Look," I said.

My mother looked. She was standing near the stove, an eighty-year-old woman in running shoes, and this is what happened. Her hands fell open at her sides, her face yielded, her shoulders dropped. She said with unfeigned rapture, "I love yah. Oh, I love yah."

Then she took my face between her hands and kissed me on both cheeks, and I was almost overcome.

I kept myself in hand by recounting a failure. The last time I attempted a lemon meringue pie, I confessed, I overdid the lemon rind and it was so bitter I was the only one who ate it.

"Oh, I've had some disasters," my mother said with feeling.

Then, a wry shake of her head toppled my lifelong view of her as the last and best of the pioneers. "You want to know how to make a sure-fire lemon meringue pie? Buy a lemon pie mix and add the juice of one lemon and the grated rind. It never fails."

I could not believe my ears. "You use a package now!"

"It's always a hit. Everybody loves it."

I stared at her humour-filled face. She was a radiant old woman. The youthful prettiness had returned after her four children left home and she was free to follow her artistic dreams. Every time I saw her, I found myself drinking her in, entranced by her nut-brown skin and bright, bright eyes. She had had her share of flops. Now she was bent on hits.

"Then that's what I'll do from now on," I vowed, dumbfounded by how wrong I had been. It occurred to me that I was always wrong. Even when I was fundamentally right, I was wrong. Knowing this filled me with pleasure and relief. I told my mother that the cookbooks were wrong too when they directed us to add the lemon juice *after* you take the filling off the element.

We were like Hemingway men comparing fishing tips, except our terrain was the uneven ground of kitchen temperament and wishful thinking, and of dubious, not to say competitive, domestic achievement. How could I have forgotten that my rigid mother was also a sly dog?

We had dinner outside on the back porch, where an evening breeze blew in from the Rideau River. I brought out the pie and served a slice to my mother, not too large, and to my father, larger, and then to Mark and the kids and myself. We ate the whole pie. It was not restaurant-solid, yet it was firm; the meringue could have been higher and I wished it was; but it tasted delicious, potent with lemon. My parents were neither over-effusive nor understated. They were genuinely, believably appreciative.

A year passed and my story gained a triumphant footnote. In June I entered the pie contest in the annual neighbourhood picnic. Getting out my biggest pie plate, I filled it with a lemon meringue pie made from not one, but two packages. I used a sharp knife to carve my creation into sixteen narrow slices, stuffing the ballot box by increasing the number of potential votes. In the end my pie got eleven votes; the runner-up (a smaller, outrageously rich concoction of strawberries and whipped cream) got ten. That evening I telephoned my mother and we were shameless in our mutual approval.

ACKNOWLEDGEMENTS

This book started out as an oversized haystack. Its first readers were my in-house editing team of Fried and son, Mark and Ben, who made many excellent suggestions and improvements. My always astute and invaluable agent, Jackie Kaiser, then convinced me to take the brutal but necessary step of lopping off the front of the manuscript. Then my Canadian editor, Martha Kanya-Forstner, brought her marvellous shaping vision to bear and found the Hays in the haystack, Jean and Gordon, and much that was beside the point fell away. I am deeply grateful—on my knees, in fact—to all of the above.

My thanks to Shaun Oakey for his deft copyediting. To Kelly Hill for her elegant design. And to Ashley Dunn, publicist supreme and my personal Rock of Gibraltar.

Thank you to the editors of *Ottawa Magazine* and *Elle Canada*, where three of these chapters appeared in altered form.

Special thanks to Christopher MacLehose and Katharina Bielenberg of MacLehose Press, and to Nathaniel Marunas of Quercus U.S. for their insights and enthusiastic support.

Finally, deep gratitude to my brothers and sister, Stuart, Alex, and Jeannie, to my children, Sochi and Ben, and to my husband, Mark, for memories, clarifications, and fellow feeling, and especially for their helping and steadying hands with the care of my parents.

A NOTE ABOUT THE TYPE

The body of *All Things Consoled* has been set in a digitized form of
Bembo, a typeface based on an old-style Roman face that was used for
Cardinal Bembo's tract De Aetna in 1495. Bembo was first cut by
Francisco Griffo in the early sixteenth century. The Lanston Monotype
Corporation of Philadelphia brought the well-proportioned letter-
forms of Bembo to North America in the 1930s.